THE CAT AND MAN

GILLETTE GRILHÉ

THE CAT
AND MAN

Photo research:
Denise Blum and
Ingrid de Kalbermatten

G. P. Putnam's Sons • New York

G.P. Putnam's Sons
200 Madison Avenue
New York, N.Y. 10016

Published in the United States of America, 1974
© 1974 by Office du Livre, Fribourg (Switzerland)
SBN: 399-11385-1
Library of Congress Catalog Card Number: 74-78403

Printed in Switzerland

CONTENTS

THE CAT THROUGH THE AGES

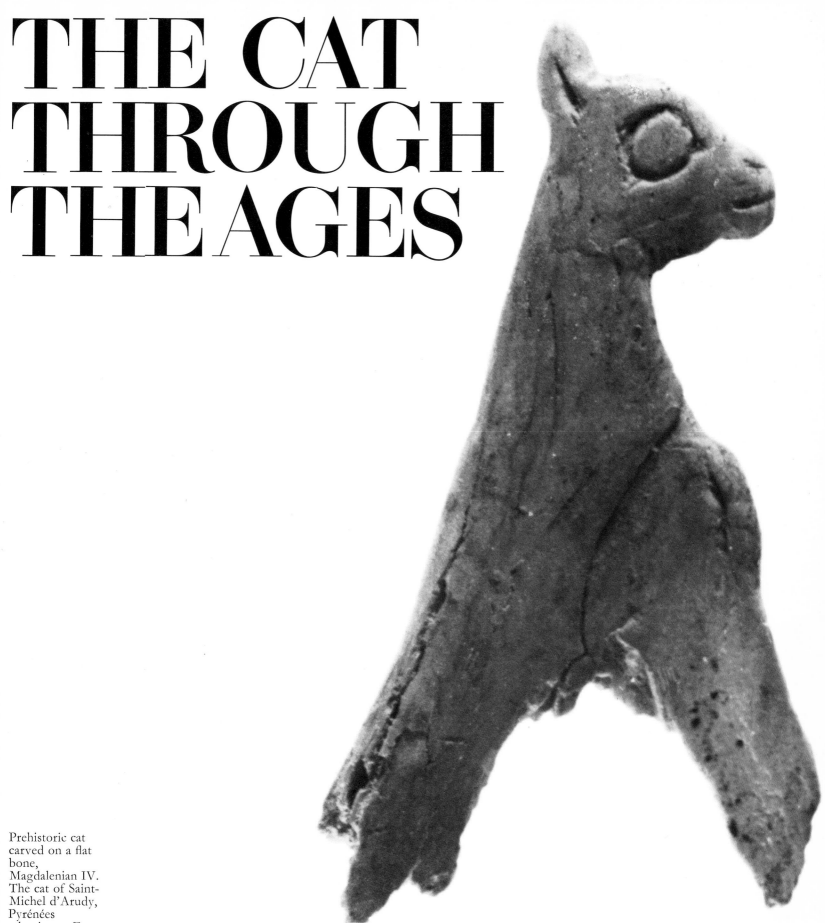

Prehistoric cat carved on a flat bone, Magdalenian IV. The cat of Saint-Michel d'Arudy, Pyrénées atlantiques, France.

INTRODUCTION

drawn into his aura of mystery. However, they never tried to go beyond this point. Works devoted to cats present them to us more often than not in an accumulation of incidents and anecdotes which our dreams and imagination can play upon as they wish. It is difficult to find in them any precise explanation of the extremely close rapport that has linked the animal to man in the course of the various phases of their common history.

The cat is a feline, and therefore carnivorous. But, being small, he has never represented a mortal danger to man, while his skill at preying upon the hosts of rodents made him an obviously desirable ally as soon as man began to store grain.

Thus, from the very outset in prehistoric times we come across the ambiguity of the feelings the cat has inspired. Wherever man was a hunter the cat was a rival that had to be eliminated and even today, a situation of this type persists with wild cats, still to be found in various parts of the world.

Where, however, man was a farmer, the cat became the providential watchman over the graneries, and, as such, had special rights in the home, where his

The cat becomes man's ally against rodents. Drawing from a *Bestiary* in the Library of the University of Cambridge, U.K.

The cat was, on occasions, the rival of the huntsman. Brussels Tapestry.

It may seem odd that we should have undertaken this study into the history of the civilization of an animal as simple, familiar and obvious as the cat. If we have done so, it is not to emulate various noted authors who have written fondly and indeed lyrically of the cat but because this animal, so beloved of many of our contemporaries, has, in the course of the centuries, been treated in the most diverse and fluctuating ways, and aroused the most contradictory attitudes and beliefs.

Loathed or adored, however, the cat has never left man indifferent. Poets and artists have been loudest in their praise of his silent presence, his eclecticism and his independence. Attracted by the strange fixity of the cat's look they were intuitively

8

This contemporary
mosaic catches the
full power of the
cat's silent gaze.
Constantin
Grichting, after a
drawing by Suzanne
Grichting-Le
Bourgeois.

The cat was believed in antiquity to be a *Genius Loci. Jupiter and Mercury received by Philemon and Baucis* by Jacob Jordaens.

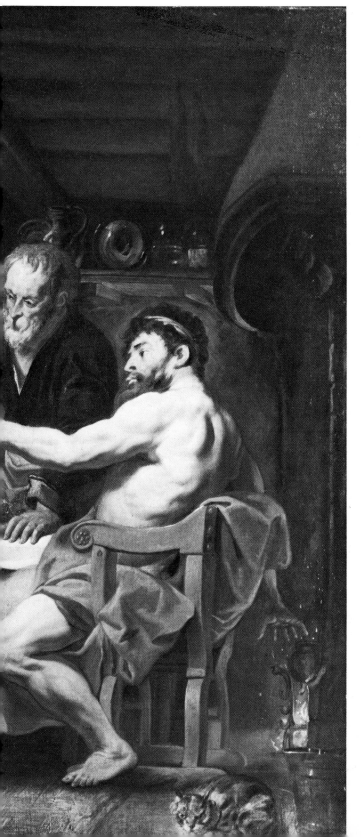

feline qualities were to give him his elevated position, different from that of the dog, but no less privileged. The dog is the recognized 'watchdog' that bows and scrapes before its master, suffering in humility his every whim. The cat on the other hand, will never be servile, however attached he may be to his master. His pride forbids him to obey, or—if he does—he will do so only when a sufficient amount of time has elapsed after the order to make the full weight of his disdain felt, reacting only as a gesture of condescension.

So that, after finding the cat deified by the Egyptian peasant, we next meet him incarnating, in classical antiquity, the role of the protecting genius of the house, a mysterious function for which other aspects of his feline nature make him admirably equipped.

Thus also, he became a symbol of independence, of liberty. We all know the properties of static electricity of the cat's skin. In the course of the thousands of years during which man was, far more than we are, subject to the influence of invisible and occult powers, it was this forceful presence of the cat that the Ancients sensed, considering it a *genius loci*, a living force, immobile, silent, beside the autumn fireside.

But that very silent force itself, the glint in the cat's look, could just as well inspire fear and hate, when linked with the age-old peasant's hatred of the poacher, against the marauding cat who destroyed game. The power and force of the cat's look is like that of a magician. It only needed Christianity, confusing paganism with witchcraft and viewing both as the machinations of Satan, for the cat, so often adored by women, to be given the role of the incarnation of a witch, and martyred as such.

These fears have vanished in modern times. The cat's role as a rat-catcher has luckily ensured his survival. In millions of homes today throughout the world, his beauty and his autonomy ensure him a significant place in the household.

I THE ORIGIN OF THE WILD AND THE DOMESTIC CAT

The cat, the only truly domestic carnivore apart from the dog, was slow in linking its destiny with man. The modern, domestic varieties apparently are not direct descendants of the indigenous wild cat, only a few specimens of which still remain in the forests. It is worth noting that the indigenous European wild cat was rarely, if ever, domesticated, the majority of our domestic cats coming principally from Africa.

Domestication of animals started in the Mesolithic period with the dog as an auxiliary to the hunter. Other domestications followed later after the start of the Neolithic period, when man first began to farm, to cultivate the fields and herd cattle.

The history of the taming of the cat has been studied less than that of other domestic animals. Until the time of Georges Cuvier (1769–1832), it was believed that the wild cat (*felis sylvestris*) was the ancestor of the domestic cat, because the tame ones were similar in shape, though smaller and finer because of their environment. However, Linnaeus in 1746 suspected that *felis catus* was of foreign origin and this was confirmed by the Dutch naturalist Coenraad Jacob Temminck, who first established the difference between the species in his *Monographie de Mammalogie* (1841). He observed that the wild cat possesses a more powerful body, longer legs and broader head, pricked ears and rather larger eye, veined, with a greenish yellow iris, and a short club-like tail spreading out in a tuft at the top. The wild cat mates only once a year and has a slightly longer gestation period (sixty-eight days) than the domestic cat. It is possible to cross the wild and domestic cat, but the progeny are delicate, generally die very young, and never produce a second generation.

The first cats are supposed to have appeared in the Eocene period with the Miacides mammals. Marcellin Boule, the French paleontologist, believed that *felis zitelli*, one of the last of their number, resembled our modern domestic cat both in size and appearance. Nevertheless it seems more likely that the domestic cat is the result of a long, progressive domestication of a wild feline from either Libya or Nubia. In fact, although bones of dogs, deer and cattle have all been found, there is absolutely no trace of the presence of the domestic cat either in the 'kitchen-midden' (prehistoric settlements) culture of Scandinavia, or among the débris of the lake-dwellers or among the other fossil remains of proto-history.

Historically the cat makes its appearance at the beginning of Egyptian civilization. Many accurate paintings and perfectly preserved mummies have survived in which we are able to recognize the 'gloved' cat *(felis maniculata)*, now officially classified as *felis libyca forster*, or *felis ocreata gmelin*. This is thought to be the most likely ancestor of the European *felis domestica*, because, unlike other species, it is easy to tame and breeds well in captivity. In this connection Georg Schweinfurth, the German Egyptologist, records that the Niam-Niam, a tribe from eastern Sudan, have no domestic cats as we understand it, but that they use 'gloved' cats, a sub-species of African wild cat: children catch these cats and tame them quickly by fastening them near the huts. When they are released, the cats stay in the vicinity of the village and rid it of all the small rodents.

Philology also provides a clue to the zoological and historical facts surrounding cats. Raoul Pictet discovered that in every European language the word cat has no Aryan derivation, but is relatively recent, coming either from the Low Latin, *cattus* or *catus*, or from the Byzantine Greek *katos*. The term *cattus* is itself derived from Syrian *gato*, in Arabic *qitt*, which in turn comes from African languages, constituting another argument in favor of hypothetical African origin for the primitive domestic cat. The difference between *felis* and *cattus*, it has been suggested, is that *cattus* should really be applied only to the domestic cat imported from Egypt.

Europe was late in acquiring the domestic cat. Apparently the Greeks introduced it first after

The European wild cat is almost extinct. Today's domestic cat is not descended from it, as is often supposed, but originated in Africa. Engravings from *Œuvres complètes* by Buffon, Paris, 1835.

Rare wall-painting
of a cat (Paleolithic:
between Solutrean
and Middle
Magdalenian) in
Gabillou Cave,
Dordogne, France.

The cat makes its
first recorded
appearance in the
early Nile
civilization. Cairo
Museum of
Antiquities.

stealing it from the Egyptians. The rarity of these domestic cats gave them a certain value which they retained for many centuries throughout Europe. In France the *Livre des Mestiers* of 1268 indicates that the tax payable in Paris for pelts of wild cats was not the same as that for 'house cats, called hearth or fireside cats.' In England the animal remained a luxury for a long time, as is evidenced by the strict laws pronounced on the subject and the heavy penalties meted out to cat-thieves (cf. Chapter VII). These laws are a further proof of the foreign, exotic origin of the domestic cat, because Great Britain, like the rest of Europe, had plenty of its own wild cats at that time. It would appear, then, from the foregoing, that the European wild cat was not considered, and is not, the ancestor of its domestic counterpart.

Wild or domestic, however, the outline of the cat's special, unchanging personality grows clearer in the course of its long relationship with man.

The word 'cat'
originated in
African languages,
and was
transmitted through
Arabic, Syrian,
Greek and Latin.
Tavoli di animali by
Ulisse Aldrovandi,
Vol. V, c. 33.
University Library
of Bologna.

Felis alter Syriacus pauacis
multis Insignitus.

The cat can be strange, haunting, mysterious, but he always has a strong personality: *Le Chat* by Picasso. Etching for Buffon's *Histoire naturelle*.

II AGRARIAN RITES AND THE CAT

Some of the beliefs and human attitudes towards the cat may possibly date from the period before it was domesticated. It is therefore pertinent to ask whether the peasants' dislike of the wild cat was in some way responsible for its role in witchcraft during the Middle Ages. Ancient harvest rites which used an animal as the 'Corn-Spirit' may also go far back to the Neolithic period, before the Oriental domestic cat had been introduced.

The animal traditionally pursued by the reapers, who cut off its paws with the last swathe, could be a bear, a fox, a dog, a hare, a cock or even a cat, depending on the country. It is interesting that apart from the cock and the dog, these animals were never domesticated. It is therefore probable that the wild cat was involved in a mythical role.

Wilhelm Mannhardt and Sir James Frazer, the British historian, made extensive studies of these popular traditions, which were still common all over Europe during the last century. About forty years ago, C. W. von Sydow and Arnold Van Gennep, the true founder of the science of ethnology in France, challenged their antiquity, but ethnological studies in Eastern Europe have since confirmed it. The following are examples of peasant-rites in which the cat takes part.

In Russia the cat was thought to be an incarnation of the Corn Spirit and the *Mokshans* buried a black cat in the trough of the furrows. At Napolnoïe, an old man carrying a black cat walked ahead of the young bachelors who held the plough. A similar rite is found in Guyenne, Labourd and Béarn in south-western France where a cat was buried alive to clear weed-infested ground, or at the foot of an apple tree to increase its yield.

An old man carried the cat—the Corn-Spirit—and young unmarried men held the plough, clearly depicting the death of the god: the old man represents death, the Beyond, the source of all wealth, followed by the young man full of promise personify-

The cat as an incarnation of the Corn Spirit. In North Africa, a piece of corn is hung behind the door to bring good luck; the luck is doubled if the cat nibbles it.

ing the resurrection. They represent the age-group responsible for the fertility of the next sowing.

The Corn-Spirit sometimes takes the form of a cat in Germany: near Kiel and in Thuringia children are warned not to go into the corn fields 'because the Cat sits there.' In some parts of Silesia, when cutting the last swathe, they say: 'The Cat is caught,' and at threshing the man who gives the last stroke is called 'the cat.' The reaper who cuts the last corn is enveloped in rye or corn stalks and green withes and is furnished with a long plaited tail. Sometimes he is accompanied by a man similarly dressed who is called the (female) cat. Their duty is to run after people they meet and beat them with a long stick. It is not their intention to hurt their victims, but simply to pass on to them the fertility of the Corn-Spirit.

The same customs were found in Lorraine, Franche-Comté, Picardy, Dauphiné, Lyonnais, and many other French provinces where the completion of an important task on the farm, either haymaking or harvest, was called 'taking' or 'killing the cat.' The cat was said to be fat or lean depending on the crop. At Briançon, in Dauphiné, at the start of reaping, a cat was decked out with ribbons, flowers and ears of corn, and called the Cat of the Ball-Skin. If a reaper was wounded at his work, they made the cat lick the wound. At the close of the reaping, the cat was again decked out as before; then they danced and made merry. When the dance was over, the girls solemnly stripped the cat of its finery.

Near Amiens, when the harvest was nearly done people said: 'They are going to kill the Cat'; and when the last corn was cut they killed a cat in the farmyard. At threshing-time, in other parts of France, a live cat was placed under the last bundle of corn to be threshed, and struck dead with the flails. Then it was roasted and eaten.

This ceremony marked the symbolic death of the spirit of vegetation, and is reminiscent of the Cat of the Ball-Skin ritual at Briançon. The symbol remains more or less the same: the Corn-Spirit has to be killed in order to rise stronger than ever, an animistic idea dating perhaps from the Paleolithic period.

The sacred nature of the ear of corn, symbol of eternal life, has survived the centuries. The following legend from Lorraine associates it with the cat:

'In olden times the ear of corn covered the stalk from top to bottom. One day the Lord, weary of man's iniquity, decided to deprive him of this precious food-plant as a punishment. "Henceforth the corn you grow will supply you with straw only," he said. "There will be no more corn." One of the angels, hearing these words, cried out: "Lord is the cat also responsible for the crimes of its master?" "No," replied the Lord. "Then we pray you to leave the part on the end of the stalk that man has always reserved for him." The Lord agreed, and from that day on the stem of the corn was long, the ear short.' Thus, according to the legend, we owe our daily bread to the cat.

As the incarnation of the Corn-Spirit, the cat had a prophetic role evident in several Flemish rites. Until the year 1818, it was customary to throw a live cat from the top of the church tower at Ypres on the second Wednesday in Lent. The cat usually fell on its feet—a good omen for the next harvest. More than a hundred years later, in 1938, the people of Ypres revived this secular tradition by throwing symbolic cats from the belfry to the crowd below. The *Kattefest*, discontinued during the last war, started again in 1946, but is now merely a piece of folklore.

Other parts of Flanders also had 'Cat Fairs' in the spring. Pealing bells announced the ceremony. Ropes were tied from one house to another with clay pots slung on them, each containing a cat decorated with multi-coloured ribbons fastened to the cords. Men in bullock-carts broke the pots with

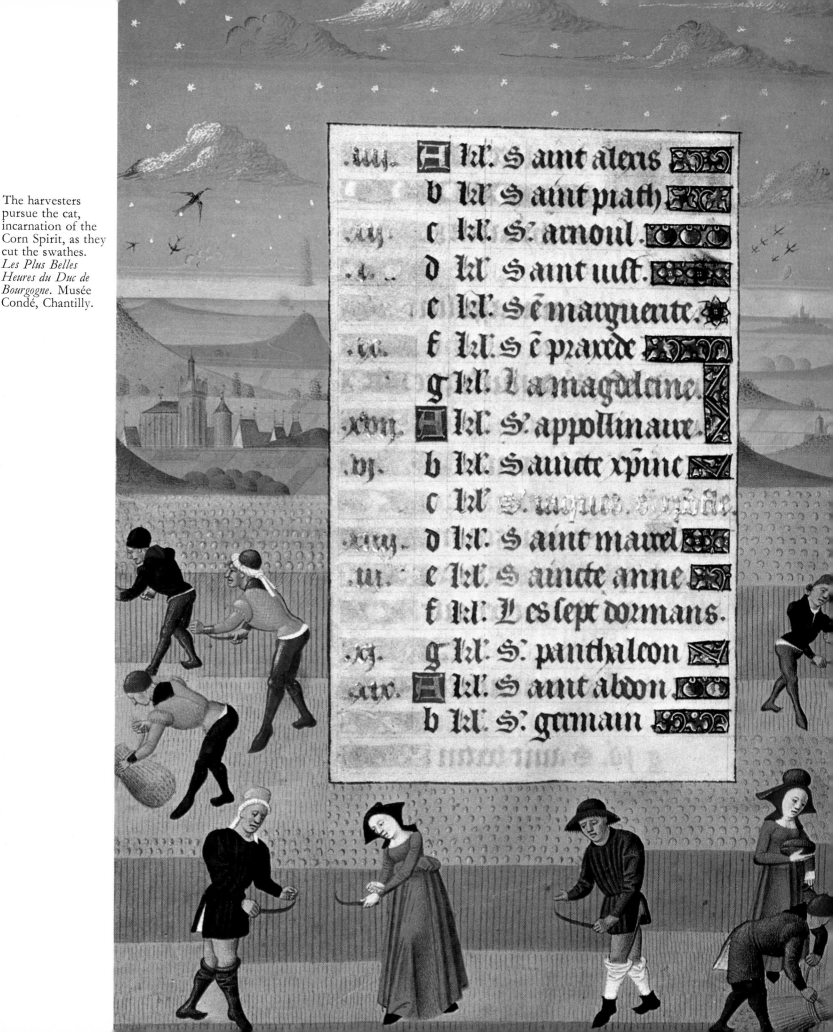

The harvesters pursue the cat, incarnation of the Corn Spirit, as they cut the swathes. *Les Plus Belles Heures du Duc de Bourgogne.* Musée Condé, Chantilly.

Nowadays the *Kattefest* (Cat Feast) at Ypres is only a symbolic festival.

Cutting the last swathe was called 'killing the cat.' In some districts of Europe, a live cat was actually killed afterwards. *June: Harvest* by Benedetto Antelami. Baptistery of Parma.

It fell to the Town Fool to throw a live cat from the Tower of Ypres, a custom that died out at the First World War.

a blow as they passed beneath. The animal thus freed was left hanging from the rope and the men had to try to remove the ribbons, getting bitten and scratched for their pains. Finally the cords were cut and the cat fell to the ground to be killed by the tumultuous crowd.

This killing of the cat no longer held any element of sacrifice: it was more like those popular feasts during which the populace simply took pleasure in killing the wretched animals, as we shall see in Chapter VI.

III THE CAT GOD OF ANCIENT EGYPT

It must have seemed to Neolithic man something of a miracle that the most dangerous of all Paleolithic man's enemies—a feline—should settle down with him in the villages. In the course of time, in those same villages that saw the flowering of the Nile civilization, the cat became a sacred animal, of divine origin, like those other equally formidable creatures, the snake, the crocodile and the lion. Its importance increased down the centuries, until by the Late Period of around 1000 B.C. it had become a tutelary god throughout Egypt.

At the beginning of the fourth millennium, long before the first hieroglyphs, there were indications of deities in Egypt. At that time, the inhabitants of the Nile valley lived in tribes, each with its own god, generally personified either by an animal or a bird. Subsequently anthropomorphism developed, and finally nothing was left of the animal except its head, on a male or female body. Sometimes only the ears, or occasionally the horns, protruded from the human face to recall the god's animal origin.

A reproduction of a cat found in the famous tomb of Ti at Saqqara dates from the Old Kingdom, in the reign of the Fifth Dynasty (2563–2423 B.C.). It was not a royal dynasty, and may have been raised to the throne by priests of Heliopolis who built a temple in the same period which became a prototype for the sanctuary of Râ, where the cat was worshipped as a symbol of the Sun God. In the *Book of the Dead*, parts of which date from 3500 B.C., the cat is defined: 'I am the great cat at the pool of the Persea in Heliopolis, the one who kept watch over the guilty men during the night of the great battle at the time when the enemies of the God were destroyed.' The great solitary cat sits at the foot of the Persea, a cosmic tree, with its paw on a snake's head. In Egyptian mythology the great serpent of the nether regions, called Set or Apophis, is the symbol of evil overcome by Osiris or Râ. The religious role of the cat in the *Book of the Dead* inspired several works of

In the Later Period, Bastet, in the form of a cat, became the Tutelary Goddess of all Egypt. Musée du Louvre.

art where the animal is seen fighting with Apophis: on a magic wand discovered at Litch (Middle Kingdom, 2065–1785 B.C.) it is biting the snake. On the tomb of Sennedjem it holds a knife in its right paw and cuts off the reptile's head. Finally, we find the cat going by the name of Bastet, a goddess with the body of a woman and the head of a cat, sometimes the wife-sister and other times the daughter of Râ.

Although all the gods, goddesses, the temples of Egypt are known, very little is understood of their nature and often even less of their legends. Many surviving religious texts allude to mythological events without any explanation, because they were learned and transmitted orally from generation to generation. The myth of Osiris is the sole exception.

The demotic papyrus (in simplified script) of the Late Period (1090–1030 B.C.) is therefore exceptionally interesting because it describes the origin and nature of Bastet. The documents recount the ancient legend of the Faraway Goddess. The daughter of Râ had fled in a temper to the Nubian desert where she hid in the shape of a lioness. Her father, who needed her presence to protect him against his enemies, sent Onouris and Thot to bring her back to Egypt.

The messengers of the Sun managed to persuade her to return. On the way home she drowned her anger by bathing in the sacred waters of Philae on the southern border of Egypt, calmly adopting the form of a cat. She sailed down the Nile acclaimed by people on the banks, until she came to Bubastis, which became a holy place where periodic feasts were held in her honor. The principal episode is shown on an ostrakon from the New Kingdom (1580–1090 B.C.) —the moment when the goddess returns to her cat shape—while a picture of the temple of Dakkeh shows Thot pleading with the raging goddess.

In the 5th century B.C., Herodotus reported that an immense crowd of worshippers from all parts of the country used to gather at Bubastis for the great annual feast. Men and women sailed down the Nile, playing music and dancing. They pulled in to the bank at every village and became very excited during the religious demonstrations. On arrival at Bubastis they celebrated with great sacrifices.

The cat, symbol of the beneficient Sun, severs the head of the serpent Apophis, symbol of Evil. British Museum.

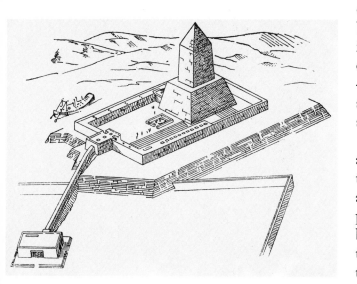

In the temples of Râ, cats were worshipped as symbols of the Sun-God. Reconstitution of a Sun Temple.

The pacified
Goddess dons her
cat-likeness again.
Staatliche Museen,
Berlin.

Those people were following the path of the Cat-Goddess. Like her they travelled in a boat down the river, saluting the villages that had acclaimed her. Thus the goddess was symbolically brought home every year, to assure the people's welfare by keeping watch over the Sun-God. The legend, in which Râ demands the return of his daughter to defend him against his enemies, confers on her the role of

Bastet sailed down the Nile in a barge, acclaimed by crowds all the way along the river on both banks.
Musée du Louvre.

Guardian Spirit. Bastet assumed her protective role extending it to the family, the house, city and tribe. Râ was the Sun, the Giver of Life, and his enemies were darkness and evil. Hence Bastet was supposed to save mankind from contagious diseases and evil spirits.

The Egyptians worshipped Bastet as the Lady of the Sky. They dedicated their new-born infants to her, hanging a portrait medallion of the cat-headed goddess round their necks. After its consecration, the child's head was shaved and the hair placed on a balance and weighed against pieces of gold. The money was then given to the custodian of the cat to which the baby had just been dedicated, to help towards its keep. At adolescence, a cat's silhouette was tattooed on the child's arm to attract the gifts of Bastet. This union was confirmed periodically at official ceremonies by injecting the child with drops of blood from the sacred animals of the Temples.

The Egyptians
float down the Nile
in a barge to
Bubastis.
Turin Museum.

Above:
The cat occupied an important place in the Egyptian household.
Below:
The cat symbolizes the Corn Spirit.

Here Bastet in a wall-painting (third from the left) helps the reapers and thereby ensures a good harvest for them. Musée du Louvre.

Bastet also was credited with virtues as healer. Statue covered with magic formulae belonging to a priest of Bastet. Musée du Louvre.

Among her other names, Bastet was also called the Goddess of Love in Egypt. Lovers invoked her aid; women with the appearance and graceful movements of a cat were much sought and admired. It was said that Cleopatra's irresistible charm came from her resemblance to a cat.

The Egyptians kept the best place in their house for the cat: he was the Household God. They watched unceasingly over the animal's well-being and if by any chance a cat died under its master's roof, all the members of the household shaved their eyebrows in mourning. The fear of a cat dying at home was so great that if a house caught fire the inhabitants were more intent on saving the cat than putting out the flames. If an animal was burned to death they covered their faces with soot and ran about the village beating their breasts, their clothing in disarray.

If Polyen or Poluainos, the sixth-century Greek philosopher, is to be believed, their anxiety was strong enough to influence political events. In 525 B.C. Pelusium was occupied by an Egyptian garrison besieged by Cambyses, the Persian king, son of Cyrus the Great. Knowing the people's devotion to cats, Cambyses ordered his soldiers to carry cats instead of shields in the attack. When the Egyptians saw this, they chose to surrender rather than run the risk of hurting a single cat, because they believed that a man who killed a cat, voluntarily or not, was doomed to die. The people would close in around the man who had done so and stone him to death, throwing his battered corpse to the Manes, the deified soul, of the creature they worshipped.

One unfortunate Roman paid with his life for ignorance of this cat-worship: he contemptuously killed a cat in the land of the Pharaohs, and neither Ptolemy the king, nor the fear of Roman reprisals, sufficed to save him from the fury of the Egyptians.

The function of a protective spirit was to watch over the life of his protégé and keep him safe. Isis,

Demeter and Earth-Mother personified the fertile land of Egypt. Her principal temple was at Philae where she was still worshipped until the 6th century A.D. We have already seen that it was at Philae that Bastet soothed her anger by bathing in the waters of the Nile and adopted her cat-form, thus ensuring the sun's warmth to ripen the harvest. Influenced by the Earth-Mother the cat became a Corn-Spirit, exemplified by a small statue of Bastet in the Louvre with the engraving 'Plants of the two Kingdoms.' The Egyptians believed dreams to be messages from the gods, and a treatise on the interpretation of dreams, dating from the Middle Kingdom (2065–1785 B.C.), is: 'If you dream of a large cat, you will have a rich harvest.'

Herodotus also recounts the behavior of the pilgrims as they floated down the Nile to Bubastis during the annual feast of the Cat-Goddess: 'Whenever they pass a town they bring the boats close inshore and then, while some of the women continue (playing instruments, dancing and clapping their hands), others shout and jeer at the townswomen, while still others dance, stand upright, pulling up their skirts; and so they go on in every village on the river bank.' This rite ensured the fertility of the river villages.

Toward 950 B.C., Sheshong, Chief of the Lioyen, seized power and founded the Twenty-Second Dynasty. He made Bubastis his capital (derived from *Per Bast*, the transcription of which means 'House of Bastet'). From that point on the daughter of Râ, formerly only a local goddess from the 18th Nome (province) of Lower Egypt, was raised to the highest rank and became the great goddess of the kingdom. This was her apogee: her protection now extended beyond the individual, the home or the city to the entire country.

Bastet was presented to her Egyptian worshippers in the form of a cat-headed woman. She is usually depicted standing holding a *sistrum* (an ancient form

Cleopatra's charm was held, in her Roman as in her Egyptian form, to reside in her resemblance to a cat. Bibliothèque Nationale, Paris, and Cairo Museum.

of rattle) in her right hand, and in her left, at waist-level, a device consisting of a large crescent-shaped pectoral surmounted by the head of a lioness and a sun-disk. She carried a small basket in the crook of her left arm.

The *sistrum* is a rattle made of a curved frame extended to form a handle and joined by four moving lappets which vibrate when shaken. The four lappets symbolize the four elements: fire, earth, air and water. The faces of Isis and Nephtys are engraved above them. 'The Egyptians intend the faces to represent birth and death, because birth and death

At Philae, Bastet is pacified in the waters of the Nile, and takes on her cat-form, thereby symbolizing the beneficient rays of the sun.

Bastet carrying a *sistrum* (percussion instrument), on which the figure of a cat sometimes replaces the usual four lappets. British Museum.

are the changes and movements to which the four elements are subjected,' according to Plutarch. A cat is carved on the end of the instrument. Sometimes the four lappets are replaced by a figure of a cat, as though the animal alone controlled the four elements. The *sistrum* in Bastet's hand symbolizes joy, music and dance. That is why the pilgrims on their way to Bubastis were merry, and played instruments and danced; they were paying homage to the personality of the goddess.

The medallion bearing the lion's head and sun disk is a reference to Bastet's mythical origin and relation to the sun. Her worshippers may have placed grains of corn in her little basket—we have already noticed that the goddess held the key to a rich harvest.

The cat's role of guardian extended beyond the grave: many female funerary figures bear the inscription TECHAU (meaning THE CAT), sign of the patronage of the goddess Bastet. In the necropolis of Thebes on the tomb of King Hana (Eleventh Dynasty), the king's favourite cat, Bouhaki, lies at his feet.

Bastet is also to be seen presiding over funerary rites on an Egyptian papyrus of the New Kingdom (1580–1090 B.C.); and Nephtys, who when seen on sarcophagi, acted as Protector of the dead, is found on the *sistrum* of the cat-goddess.

In common with Mother-Goddesses throughout antiquity, the Cat-Goddess Bastet was a Guardian Spirit. It is possible that this religious function may have travelled from Egypt into the traditions of Africa. After the second millennium B.C., Pharaohs of the New Kingdom are known to have sent boats round Africa. And again some tribes, like the Bantu and the Masai, originated on the Upper Nile. Perhaps this explains why the cat occupies such an important position in tribes which believe in transmigration of souls after death. Some small tribes also regard the cat as the familiar spirit of individuals, the family

or the tribe. An example is the Bantu Ba-Ronga tribe: they believe that the life of the whole clan is incarnate in a cat, as shown by the legend of Titichane.

'A young man bought a wife called Titichane. The girl's parents said to her "Take an elephant with you." She refused, replying: "Where would I keep it? There are no forests near my fiancé's village." So then they suggested an antelope. Once more she replied: "Where would I put it? It would be better if you gave me your cat." Her parents would not hear of it. "You know perfectly well that all our lives depend on this cat." The daughter insisted, saying: "Oh well, never mind. I might be very unlucky if you refused."

Bastet's worshippers placed corn in her basket so that she would bring about a good harvest. Musée du Louvre.

Bastet—the body of a woman with the head of a cat— holding the *sistrum* in one hand, with four cats at her feet. British Museum.

'So they handed over the cat and she left. She made a little enclosure for the animal without telling her husband. One day before she left for the fields, Titichane told the cat it could go into the hut and eat the porridge left in the pot. As soon as she had gone the cat crept out of its shelter and went into the hut. When it had finished off the porridge it took down the husband's warrior-headdress and the belt decorated with tails and little bells, put them on, and then began to dance and sing:

O, O Titichane, where have you gone to, Titichane?
You have gone!
Go! Go! Go!

'Then, fearing that he would be discovered wearing the husband's belt and headdress, he quickly took them off and went back to his own place.

'During the next few days he repeated the performance, and soon Titichane's husband heard about the strange goings-on in his house and resolved to hide behind the door. The cat, all unsuspecting, went into the hut, ate up the food and began to sing:

O, O Titichane. Where have you gone to, Titichane?
My belly is full
How good I feel!

Whereupon the husband shot him with an arrow, the cat fell dead and all the plumes of the warrior-headdress lay scattered on the ground.

'At that very moment out in the fields where she was working, Titichane felt a shock and cried faintly: "Someone has killed me in the village." Crying, she came home, sat down at the threshold of the hut and said to her husband. "Wrap the body of the cat in a mat, I will carry him." The man did as he was bid because she dare not look upon the cat lest she should die. She laid the bundle on her shoulders and set off for her own village, her husband walking behind.

'When she got there she placed her burden on the ground in the centre of the village. A woman came to her and said: "We offered to give you an elephant.

Bastet, bearing the Cross of Life on her arm, presides at funeral rites: in this case, she leads Death to be judged by Osiris. Papyrus of the XXI Dynasty. Cairo Museum.

You refused. We offered you an antelope. You refused. Don't you realize you have killed us all now?" Then the whole village gathered at the spot. "That's the end of us—the Cat-tribe! Let her be the first—her!" So they unrolled the mat, and one after another went and looked upon the cat, whereupon they fell dead. After the last one had died, the son-in-law fastened the great gate of the village with thorn bushes so that no one would ever go in again, whereupon he left and went home. The corpses rotted away. He told his friends how, in killing the cat, he was now responsible for killing all those people, because their lives depended on the cat. That was how he came to lose what he had paid for his bride and could not claim it back because everyone concerned had died.'

IV   THE CAT AS TUTELARY GENIUS

IN CLASSICAL ANTIQUITY

At the start of the third millennium, a time which witnessed the first Pharaohs, a brisk trade existed between Egypt and the Phoenician cities. Consequently myths travelled from one to the other, and especially to Byblos. During the excavations conducted there in 1937, the French archaeologist Claude Schaeffer discovered in a sanctuary one of the largest sacrifices ever found—more than three hundred animals—including some cats—lying in natural positions in earthenware jars.

Except for Byblos, the ancient Middle East seems to have ignored the cat completely. There are no archaeological or documentary traces of its existence. But Greek mythology reserved a considerable place for the cat: Apollo, trying to frighten his sister, created the lion. Artemis in turn made the cat. Apollo was a sun god; Artemis personifies, among other things, the moon. This was the foundation of a legend that the moon had given birth to a cat. Despite this lunar aspect, the cat in the form of a lion still signifies the sun. The moon, after all, gets her light from the sun. Later the Greeks were to identify Bastet with Artemis, and the Romans did the same with Diana.

Herodotus translates cat by the Greek word *ailouros*. However, another Greek word, *gale*, is translated sometimes as 'cat' sometimes as 'weasel.' If *gale* really means cat we find it in the *Batrachomiomachos* (attributed to Homer), where it is described as a 'very large cat extremely hostile to the ratty tribe.' This author suggests that the Greeks stole the cats, as well as all their scientific knowledge, from the Egyptians. At any rate cats had a market value

Egyptian lapis-lazuli cat. Musée du Louvre.

in fifth-century Greece. The Boetian in Aristophanes's *Archanians* (425 B.C.) mentions a cat among all the other good things, ducks, waterfowl and eels from Lake Copaïs found in the market. They also appear in Aesop's fables (6th century B.C.), where they are shown as every bit as wily as the fox, and in Callimachus's *History of the Animals* (5th century B.C.). Later, Theocritus (3rd century B.C.) describes their love of comfort and warmth in his *Dialogue of the Syracusans*. The Greek word *gale* is used here in the same way as the *Batrachomiomachos* and there seems to be no doubt as to its meaning. In the context only cats fit.

Cats were depicted much less often by the Greeks than by the Egyptians, although one cat can be found on a funerary stele from Salamis (5th century B.C.) and on a bas-relief of the Battle of Marathon (5th century B.C.), where the animal is arching its back, restrained by its master's leash. Again the cat is found on a small Tanagra vase painted in black on a red ground, which would date it at around the 6th century B.C. at the earliest.

Pliny records that contemporary Arabs (about six hundred years before the Prophet) worshipped a golden cat. This explains their subsequent esteem for the animal. They believed that cats were unsullied and that their origin must be different from other animals. They attributed to the cat a fabulous birth, which soon acquired a quasi-historical nature. 'The rats had increased so fast in the Ark that they were eating up all the animal food, regardless of others. Noah decided to get rid of them, and seeing the lion nearby, gave him a pair of bellows. The lion, taken aback, sneezed, and out of the sneeze there sprang a cat, the very first to wage war on the rats.'

In Greek mythology Artemis created the cat. . . and Apollo the lion: an example of the parallel development between the two. Museum of Ephesus and Museum of Olympus, Greece.

Cats were sold in
Greek markets like
other domestic and
small farm animals.
Terracotta from
Tanagra.

The cat and the lion are once again closely connected in this legend, as in Egypt.

While the Mohammedans have always considered the dog an impure animal, they still have the greatest respect for the cat. Mohammed even mentions his veneration in the Koran. He owned a cat called Muezza (meaning 'most fair and gentle'). One day the animal lay sleeping on the Prophet's robe when the hour of prayer was called. Mohammed chose to cut away his robe rather than disturb the animal's sleep because he did not want to upset the *Genius* watching over him.

The Romans were perfectly prepared to absorb alien gods into their pantheon. So Diana did not keep her character as goddess of light and dawn, and lady of the mountain and forest for very long. She was rapidly Hellenized and, after the introduction of Egyptian gods into the Italian peninsula, the moon goddess Diana-Artemis became one with Bastet. In the *Metamorphoses*, Ovid records that Diana con-

Dogs were compared with cats even in Classical times. National Archaeological Museum, Athens, Inv. No. 3476c.

Rare Greek funerary stele showing a cat. National Archaeological Museum, Athens, Inv. No. 715.

39

Bowl of Arcesilas.
In Greece, the cat
has found its place
beneath its master's
chair, as
previously in Egypt.

cealed herself in the form of a cat, and called her *Fele, soror Phoebi* (Cat, sister of Phoebus).

Nevertheless the role of the cat was far less important in Rome than in Egypt. It was no longer a national deity, but remained a tutelary spirit and it was in this role of guardian that it appeared on the standard of the *Felices Seniores* cohort (cat, demi, red on a gilt ground), and on the standards of the Roman legionaries (white or silver escutcheon with a cat demi, green or red).

40

The cat is supposed by the Arabs to have been created in the Ark. Tapestry showing Noah's sacrifice. Wawel Museum, Cracow.

Insignia of the Roman Company called *Ordinis Augustiis* (left); Insignia of the Cohort *Felices Seniores* (centre); Arms of the soldiers *Qui Alpine vocabuntur* (right).

In the 2nd century B.C., Republican Rome boasted a Temple of Liberty, built to the order of Tiberius Gracchus. It was supported by bronze pillars and decorated with statues. Liberty was represented by a Roman matron wearing a white robe, with a sceptre in one hand and a cap in the other. At her feet was a cat. In this case the animal appears as protector of liberty and of Roman independence.

The cat was held in less esteem in everyday Rome, although it must have had some importance since it was called a *Genius Loci* and became confused with *Lares* and *Penates*, the household gods of the ancient Romans. (*Laris* meant the house: *ad larem suum vertire* means to go home.) Its altar was the hearth, which was why the *Genius* and the family *Lares* were invoked at important ceremonies such as marriages or funerals. The bride made a sacrifice to it and gave money as she crossed the threshold. Nor was the *Genius* forgotten at funerals, for over and above the sacrifices made to the *Manes* (Shades), tributes were paid to the *Genius* to ensure that its protection would extend to the future life of the deceased.

It is in this tutelary disguise that the cat reappears in Gaul. Either it was inherited (the whole length of the Rhône and Saône valleys, from Marseilles to Langres was a depository for Egyptian artefacts), or borrowed during the Gallic Wars when the legionaries, as we have seen, sometimes carried standards or shields decorated with a cat. These facts, together with the Auxerre statuette of a cat (1st to 2nd centuries A.D.) which is probably Celtic in origin, conflict with the suggestion made by several contemporary authors that the domestic cat appeared in Europe during the 4th or 5th century A.D. at the earliest. They, however, are well in advance of some naturalists who place that date no earlier than the 9th century!

In Gaul, where images of cats are rare, there are two very important sculptured cats which prove the existence and continuous role of the animal. They are the statuette of Auxerre in the Yonne *département*, mentioned above, and the pedestal of a table from Mont Auxois (Côte d'Or *département*, and site of Alésia).

43

The first piece was found in 1856 during excavations in the suburb of Saint-Amâtre on the foundations of the old city of Autessiodorum: the figure, carved in stone, 4 7/10 inches high, represents a seated cat with a gadrooned collar round its neck. Coins excavated at the same time give us a date somewhere between the 1st century B.C. and the 2nd century A.D. This cat is reminiscent of the statuettes of glazed cats found at Byblos, which can only be Guardian Spirits.

The table pedestal was discovered in 1937 and dates from the 2nd or 3rd century A.D.: a standing frontal figure of an adolescent boy with long curling hair, bare feet (indicating a supernatural character) and smiling face, wearing a tunic pulled up in front to reveal his genitals. His tunic forms a fold on which a cat is outstretched. Both the cat's body and its feet are well drawn, and it bears its delicate head proudly, with eyes larger and more prominent than life. It wears a gadrooned collar from which hangs a little bell to frighten away evil spirits.

Here we are confronted with a double representation of the *Genius Loci*, the cat and the boy, whose gesture of lifting his tunic is self-explanatory when one recalls that the *Genius* is a fertility symbol. The nuptial bed comes under its special protection, hence its name, *Genialis*. The *Genius* embodies the force of procreation, and is a generative deity.

The Mount Auxois *Genius* carved on the table pedestal appears in its dual role as boy and cat, as though the artist wanted in this way to redouble its divine virtue. This *Genius* must without any doubt have been the Guardian Spirit of the house where the table was kept. In the same way the little Auxerre cat probably took his place among the household

Double representation of the *Genius Loci*: a figure of a cat and the features of a young boy. Musée Alise-Sainte-Reine, France.

Celtic votive figure of the 1st century B.C. to 2nd century A.D., proving the presence of the domestic cat in Gaul well before the 4th century, put forward by some authorities. Musée d'Auxerre.

The leaders of the
French Revolution
placed a cat at the
feet of the figure
of Liberty as the
Romans had before
them. *La
Constitution française
de 1793* by
Prud'hon.
Bibliothèque
Nationale, Paris.

gods of a Gallo-Roman, who would carry offerings to him each morning, as he did to the *Lares* and *Penates*.

Espérandieu, in *Recueil général des bas-reliefs de la Gaule romaine*, describes several funerary steles and shows children holding a cat in their arms. These steles are done in the Celtic style predominant in Gaul until the 3rd century A.D. Only the Bordeaux Gallo-Roman stele is more recent, dating from the 4th century.

These cats are clearly all domestic, plump, well-cared-for, benevolent, allowing themselves to be stroked and held in awkward positions (as on the Bordeaux stele, for example). One explanation of the cat on children's funerary steles is that when a child died in Roman Gaul, his favourite toys were buried with him, and then the child was depicted on a stele with his pets. I believe, however, that the Gauls were reproducing the image of the *Genius* or Guardian angel of the child, so as to protect the child in the afterlife.

In fact, as we have seen, the *Genius* with the *Lares, Penates* and *Manes* (Shades) was one of the earliest divinities of Latium, and was constantly confused with the others. By definition, the *Genius* embodies the divine power of generation, and as procreator of man oversees his life until the hour of death. It appears at birth as protective spirit. It forms the personality of the child, inspires the intellectual and moral qualities of the individual and acts as a kind of incorporeal Doppelgänger. Everyone has a *Genius* more or less powerful, depending on chance. Hence the cat figured on funerary steles in its role as *Genius Loci*, although it was assimilated by now with *Manes*.

The cat continued to carry out its protective function over individuals, houses and families throughout classical antiquity, although the sacrifices made in its name were neither so ritualistic nor ceremonial as those of Egypt.

Gallo-Roman funerary stele showing a cat as the Guardian Angel for the dead child. Musée d'Aquitaine, Bordeaux.

THE CAT AS A SYMBOL OF LIBERTY AND INDEPENDENCE IN LATER TIMES

If the cat came to suggest the idea of liberty and independence it must have been because its behavior expresses instinctive resistance to submission. Unlike so many other animals now tamed and in the service of man, the cat has never been subjected to man's will. It has become accustomed to man's company without abandoning its most profound instinct— independence. Proud and determined, the cat does only what it wants.

It was principally in Europe that the cat became associated with the idea of liberty and we have seen that a cat accompanied the Statue of Liberty at Rome. It is found in the same position in an allegory of the French Constitution of 1793 painted by Prud'hon: Minerva, Law and Liberty stand together; a child leads a lion and a lamb, while a cat remains close by Liberty. At the same period a print engraved by Citizen Lingé depicts Liberty holding a broken rod, its point a Phrygian cap; at her side is a cornucopia and at her feet a cat. We know that the Phrygian cap is a symbol of authority, justice and independence. The Statue of Liberty in Rome also holds a cap in her hands.

Tradition, the very substance of civilization, is never completely lost. Sometimes when a tradition has lain dormant for a long time it only requires a shock to bring it to life again. The French Revolution provided the impetus that rehabilitated the animal proscribed by the Church.

The leaders of the French Revolution tried to confirm the rejection of autocracy, and, by taking

The Celtic and Gallo-Roman funerary steles on pp. 44 and 47 have more than a little in common with modern figures, and attitudes of children with their pet cats. Left: *Knabe mit Katze*, 1905, by Paula Modersohn-Becker, Öffentliche Kunstsammlung, Bâle, and right, *La Fillette au Chat*, 1889, by Steinlen. Musée Petit Palais, Geneva.

the Roman Republic as their guide, were inspired by Latin works generally. They adopted the image of the cat as a living symbol of their liberation.

The cat represents independence in heraldry also. There it is no longer an attribute of Liberty but Liberty itself. The early Alans, Swabians and Burgundians 'had a cat on their standards, a creature known to dislike restraint and which therefore could be a symbol and image of Liberty,' declared Palliot in his *Vraye et parfaicte science des Armoiries* and he adds: 'Just as this animal cannot be constrained to do anything, so these people cannot be made to do anything by force, and things can only be extracted from them voluntarily: everything is done by love, not force.'

The arms of Clotilde, wife of Clovis, king of the Franks, but daughter of the king of the Burgundians, were 'a gold escutcheon, a cat, sable, killing a rat, the same.' The cat figures on only about one hundred coats of arms, but it is often 'sable' or black, although occasionally gold or silver.

Arms of Burgundy.

Arms of Clotilde,
wife of Clovis.

V CATS AND WITCHCRAFT

An Old Wives' Tale from Occitania gives credence to the nine lives of the cat, and one can almost believe it when one considers how the animal survived the appalling persecution from the Middle Ages to the beginning of the 20th century.

The fourth-century Roman emperor, Constantine, became a Christian and imposed Christianity on his subjects as the State religion. This revolutionary religious policy made the Christian Church both powerful and rich, even if it lost, perhaps, in moral values what it gained in power; the Christian Church, he persecuted, now became the persecutor.

Constantine's nephew, Julius the Apostate, preferred paganism and tried to restore it. But his success was short-lived. After his death in 363 his heirs proscribed the practice of pagan cults and forced everyone to become Christian.

The cat was still enjoying a comfortable life among churchmen at the end of the 6th century, as we know because, in 590, Pope Gregory the Great had a pet cat and a theologian called John the Deacon reported that 'he liked stroking his cat better than anything else.'

Roman Catholicism had supplanted paganism, but only among a certain class. Religions do not disappear overnight.

Constantine proclaims Christianity State Religion, while Julian the Apostate tried to restore paganism. Musée du Louvre.

When Gregory the Great was organizing the Papacy in Rome, Mohammed inspired another monotheistic religion in Arabia. It should be remembered that the cat, an object of Arab worship in Pliny's day, is described as a pure animal in the Koran, whereas the dog is impure. The cat possessed the *baraka*, or blessing, and was always well-cared-for. At Bab-el-Nasz there was a hospital for sick cats to which believers brought food. During the 19th century, the French Egyptologist Prisse d'Avennes (1807–1879) records the following story: 'When he died in about 658 of the Hegira (1280 A.D.), the Sultan of Egypt and Syria El-Daher-Beybars

left in his will a garden for homeless and needy cats. The garden was called Ghet-el-Quoath (the cats' orchard) and was close by the mosque outside Cairo. Since then, it has been sold again and again because it is supposed to be unprofitable, until after continuous neglect, it only brings in a token rent of fifteen piastres a year, which, added to a few other legacies, is used to feed the cats. The *Kadi* is responsible for managing all pious and charitable legacies and arranges for a quantity of offal and butcher's meat cut in pieces to be handed over to the *asr* in the court of Mehkemeh or Tribunal to feed all the cats in the district. As feeding time approaches, every terrace is covered with cats; you see them all round the Mehkemeh—jumping from roofs across the narrow Cairo streets fearful of missing their pittance; they come from every side, along the *moucharabeh* and the walls, spreading out into the courtyard, miaowing with desperate eagerness and fighting over the pitifully small quantity allowed for so many. The old hands gulp it down in an instant; the young cats and new arrivals dare not join in the fight and are reduced to licking the spot where the meat lay. Anyone who wants to get rid of a cat goes and loses it among the throng of this strange banquet. I have seen people bringing market baskets full of kittens.

In contemporary northern Europe the cult of Feyda, whose favourite animal was the cat, meant that it had a privileged place in every home, where it watched over the harmony of the house.

The year 962 is an important date because, as far as we know, it marked a complete change in human attitudes toward the cat, a change exemplified by the dreadful events which lasted from the Middle Ages up until quite recent times.

On the Continent, the domestic cat was an Oriental import, so it was an aristocratic, or, at the very least, and urban phenomenon. Proof is found in the Gallo-Roman funerary shafts excavated and described by Abbé Baudry at Le Bernard in Vendée, a province

52

In Church circles of the 6th century the cat was appreciated: Pope Gregory the Great, as a chronicler writes, was deeply attached to his favorite cat.

STS GREGORIVS

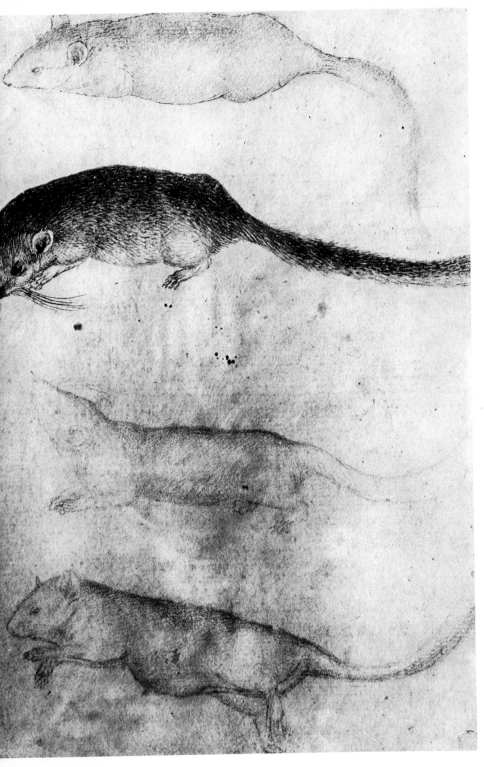

which defected from the Empire in the 2nd and 3rd centuries A.D. In the twenty-two shafts surrounding one large house, Abbé Baudry noted 'the jaws of an animal about the size of a cat' beside 'a well-preserved head of a housedog' (shaft 20), and in the female graves of shafts 6 and 7, 'the remains of a small carnivore and two other skeletons of small carnivores,' which might well be cats, identified incorrectly. Remains of dogs, however, and other domestic animals are to be found in all the shafts. This establishes that the cat was rare in Gallo-Roman country districts and was to be found only in noble houses. That this villa in western France (Le Talmondais) was really aristocratic is proved not only by the elaborate funerary shafts, but by a small detail in the first one: it contained a drinking cup made of coconut, probably from Egypt. This is less surprising when we realize that at that time the sea came very close to Le Bernard and to the site of the future castle of Talmont.

The peasant knew another kind of small cat: the wild cat, also a thief, and hence the poacher's enemy. This may be the reason for the people's bitter hatred of the feline race, and also for the belief that sorcerers, feared and suspected by farmers, could change themselves into a cat. The cat, living among pagan nobility in Gaul, was destined to be condemned by the Church because of its association with the last of the pagan cults. Had it not been for its undoubted skill as a rat-catcher, it is doubtful whether the domestic cat would have survived the Middle Ages except in its wild state.

The ceremony called 'Cat Wednesday' is mentioned in 962, probably for the first time. It took place at Metz on the second Wednesday in Lent

Returning Crusaders brought the Black Rat to Europe from Palestine. Between the 9th and 12th centuries, cats enjoyed a relatively safe period. *Rats,* by Pisanello. Musée du Louvre.

the holds of their ships, so the cat was needed to fight this new scourge, and therefore enjoyed a period of respite.

But the 13th century saw a renewal of persecution. The people of Vaud and of Albi were not only supposed to be heretics but were also accused of worshipping the devil in the shape of a black cat. To combat this heresy, Innocent III declared a crusade against the Albigensians in 1208, which totally destroyed the civilization of Languedoc. Later, in 1231, Pope Gregory XI set up the sinister Inquisition, unleashing a wave of cruelty throughout Europe. Sorcery was declared a heresy and, in the course of time, thousands of men and women, accused of practising magic and of making pacts with the devil, were burned to death.

Cats were so essential in the fight against rats that even the churches opened their doors to them. Choir stall, Cathedral of Saint-Pierre, Poitiers.

Witches and magicians with their knowledge and potions, offered competition of various sorts to the doctors. Musée du Berry, Bourges.

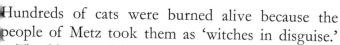

Hundreds of cats were burned alive because the people of Metz took them as 'witches in disguise.'

The history of sorcery and diabolism cannot be treated in any depth here, although perhaps it should be noted that sorcery had flourished in the Roman world. The cat does not seem to have been associated with it before the 10th century; the idea took root during the 11th and 12th centuries when Christianity was reformed after the decadence of the 10th century by the Canonical Orders created by Gerbert (Sylvester II) and by the great monastic orders. In the 11th and 12th centuries, Crusaders returned from Palestine bringing the Black Rat in

55

The Cat and the
Astrologer;
Nostradamus and
Catherine de
Medici, with the
attendant cat.

In the 14th century, the interminable struggle between the Church and paganism reached its height, particularly in France, Germany, Spain and Italy, as well as in England and Switzerland. In 1305 the Archbishop of Coventry, who acknowledged both pagan and Christian religions, barely escaped with his life. In 1324 the case against Alice Kyteler and her companions ended less fortunately: although Alice Kyteler was saved from the death sentence by her noble birth, her companions were all executed for non-compliance with the Church. These early cases were succeeded by the Inquisition of Berne, described in Nider's *Formicarius*. Here again ecclesi-astical justice seems to have punished only the humble: the important were set free. Their death would have appeared to give excessive importance to their belief.

In the 15th century, after 1408, the courts of Lorraine began a series of important trials for sorcery. Toward the end of the century, the Church, its power well entrenched, wanted to launch a final attack: in 1484 Innocent VIII published a Bull 'Against Sorcerers,' after which thousands of men and women were sent to their deaths by Christian priests on the slightest suspicion of association with the devil: to own a cat was evidence enough!

INCARNATION OF WITCHES

The modern conception of a witch took shape in the 16th and 17th centuries. The intolerance and universal suspicion engendered at that time by the wars of religion were directed not only against heresy but also against the inherited pagan beliefs. The Church found a powerful ally in the medical profession which competed with sorcerers for business, because magicians had been treated with respect and even veneration in former centuries, and in the Christian era. Men and women consulted them if they were ill, if they were unhappy or wanted to know the future. Sorcerers were received by kings, attended royal councils and gave advice on important affairs. When she was Regent of France, Catherine de' Medici could take no decision without consulting Cosimo Ruggieri, her astrologer and favourite. Other magicians and witches lived with the people, bringing them comfort and spiritual help: that was white magic. But black magic was also practised. It must be remembered that natural phenomena, now recog-

The sorcerer's familiar spirit. *Saint-Jacques le Majeur*, engraving after Brueghel the Elder. Bibliothèque Nationale de Paris.

Cats on the prowl in February were often believed to be witches. *Emotions Parisiennes*, No. 9 by Honoré Daumier. Bibliothèque Nationale, Paris.

versa, is inherent in nearly all magic systems. The idea of metempsychosis or transmigration of souls dates from prehistoric times. It is found throughout medieval Europe.

Hungarians believed that every cat between seven and twelve years old changed into a magician. In Germany cats wandering on the roofs during February were not supposed to be real cats, but witches, so that they, and black cats especially, were chased away from children's cradles.

The following are popular superstitions from the 19th century.

In Lorraine when a cat tried to avoid passing in front of a crucifix it was undoubtedly a witch in disguise. To prevent a kitten from following this wicked example, you had to cut off the end of its tail. And when you came across a fierce-looking black cat, you had to make a fork sign with your fingers: if you had guessed right and that cat was a witch it would not be able to hurt you.

Like the Djinns in Arab lore, people believed that witches borrowed the cats' likeness, preferably black, to enter houses, eat everything they wanted and cast a spell on the inhabitants. In Anjou, for example, if cat came into a bakery while the dough was being set in the baskets, the dough—so it was believed— would cook badly and make poor bread.

To achieve their metamorphoses, witches covered their bodies with a secret unguent made from the fat of a black cat. This must have been the reason a woman of Bain in Brittany crept out while her husband was asleep. One night he woke up to see his wife quietly shutting the door. Soon after he saw a huge cat come in, so, picking up an axe, he cut off one of its paws. Three days elapsed before his wife came home and she had lost one hand!

In Flanders between Bergues and Honschoote near a café called 'Het Kamje,' sounds and fierce cries of cats dancing a hellish jig were heard every evening. One evening the people shot at them with

nized as laws of nature or probability, were regarded in those days as supernatural. In prehistoric times men always believed that there were people capable of changing the course of events. They were variously called sorcerers, magicians, astrologers or prophets, depending on the community. Through all classes of society, from the king down to the humblest of his subjects, divination, dreams, fortune-telling, charms, voodoo, the belief in ghosts and evil spirits were all part of the pattern of daily life.

Belief in the metamorphosis of sorcerers into different animals, particularly into cats and vice

58

Women transformed
themselves into
cats when they
attended a witches'
sabbath.
G. Moreau:
*La Femme
métamorphosée
en Chatte.*

From the 12th
century on, the
Devil began to be
depicted as a
hideous monster.
The Devil
'Haborym'.

a gun full of salt (an antidote against witchcraft).
One of the cats fell dead, and next day there lay in
its place a beautiful lady adorned with gold and silver
jewels. She was buried with her ornaments in the
same field where she was found. Everyone believed
she was a witch.

Lawsuits of the period are full of allusions to this
kind of metamorphosis. In many cases they were
nothing but hypotheses made up by witnesses, who
had been surprised by strange animal behavior: a cat
in a stable defends itself when they try to drive it out;
the cries of cats heard in a sick room, although there
is no cat in the house; four cats go into a house and
get out although every hole is closed, 'one of them
opening locked doors in a most extraordinary way';
another cat survived in 'an inexplicable way' all
attempts to kill it; three cats mysteriously find their
way into a house, remaining hidden and impossible
to catch; others leave claw marks on beds, climb on
to a cot and cause the death of the infant; they attack
a mother, scratching her face until it bleeds; sit on a
new-born infant's face, blinding it at once, or jump
'onto the belly of a woman in labour, killing the
baby.'

Such suspicious and prodigious feats made it look
as if the mysterious cats were witches in disguise.

Sometimes the accused, during their lawsuits,
vowed that they had been the object of such muta-
tions. In his *Démonomanie* of 1580, Jean Bodin relates
that the witches of Vernon in Normandy usually
gathered in an old castle in the shape of hundreds of
cats. Four or five men resolved to spend the night
there; they were attacked by the cats and one of the
men was killed, the others wounded. Nevertheless
they managed to wound several cats which changed
back into women at once, and every one was found
to be hurt.

Witches predominate over sorcerers. In fact, if the
cat adopted a masculine form it was supposed to be
devil himself.

Until the 12th century, the Devil was depicted with a human form and without any particular physical deformity, as witness this Gospel of Charles the Bald of the 9th century. Bibliothèque Nationale, Paris.

By the 15th century,
the Devil generally
appeared in animal
form, very often
that of a cat. Goya:
Gatesca pantomima.

It will be recalled that the original Roman marriage laws made the wife her husband's chattel; and of course, Jewish society, the source of Christianity, was strongly patriarchal. So when the new religion spread into western Europe, women were excluded from the liturgy. Any priestess celebrating holy ritual was considered a pagan. Priests, bishops and Christian monks held that pagans were worshippers of the devil, given to all kinds of debauchery and perversion.

INCARNATION OF THE DEVIL

As an incarnation of a witch, Christians believe the cat to be a demon, in its Christian, pejorative sense. In classical Greece demons were the intermediaries between men and the gods. In Rome they were called the *Genius*. In repudiating the pagan gods, Christianity naturally damned their intermediaries.

The presence of the devil, the very principle of evil, coloured the whole outlook of the Middle Ages. At first he was represented in human form with no physical defects, as in the *Gospel of Charles the Bald* of the 9th century; but after the 12th century he became a hideous, ever more grotesque monster. By the 15th century he had lost his human aspect altogether and was generally represented as an animal. Dog, goat, wolf or cat were the most usual. The clergy turned the devil into a frightful body; the smallest unusual occurrence and the slightest idea in advance of its time were all the work of the devil. Most people were obsessed by the omnipresence of the devil and exorcism was used on any trivial pretext, not that it prevented collective hallucinations, individual visions, far-reaching trials and innumerable executions.

The cat was symbolically most important as an incarnation of the devil. It came to represent the powers of darkness. Diabolical activity is essentially

Cats soon became synonymous with the Devil, as with the Devil 'Bael.'

nocturnal. In the 12th century, St. Bernard compared the night with the devil. Night was the perfect image of the satanic mystique. In fact the devil lives in the shadows. By tradition he is usually depicted as black, scraggy, and hairy, with cloven hooves, claws, horns on his forehead and, often, cat's ears. Whatever

63

disguise he adopts, even the elegant form of Goethe's Mephistopheles, he still has the animal's ears. But when he appears before his worshippers, one of his favourite shapes is an aloof black cat.

He appeared like that during the 13th century to the Cathars, the people of Vaud and the Albigensians, hence their name *Catiers*. The deliberate and telling insult was directed at the Cathars because they were reputed by their enemies to worship the devil, who appeared to them in the shape of a black cat.

In important witchcraft trials the accused admitted that the devil presided over their sabbaths in the form of a big black cat. At Chelmsford in England the inhabitants believed that the devil was a cat, and Mary Tremble and Sasanna Edwards, two witches of Devonshire, confirmed it in 1682.

In *Witchcraft in Western Europe*, Margaret Murray quotes from the confession of the Guernsey witches tried in 1563: 'About three months ago' they were with 'the old woman called Colenette Gascoing in the moat lane at Coully, where there were five or six cats, one of them black and leading the others in a dance': and the same Colenette told them to kiss that cat, whereupon the aforementioned 'kissed it on the rump,' and 'Françoise Lenouff and her mother were there with Colette Salmon, the wife of the

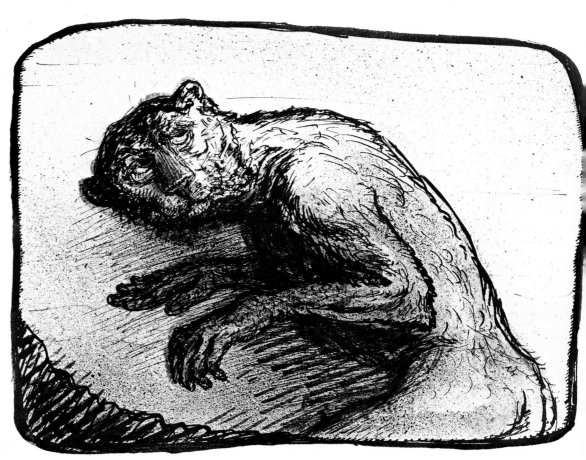

The Devil is usually depicted as hairy and black, with claws and cat's ears. Alfred Kubin: *Der Katzenmensch*. Albertina Foundation.

The Devil lurks
behind the beauty
of the Cat. Drawing
by Claude Estang.

The Cat symbolizes
the Infernal powers
of the Devil.
Capital in the
church of
Iguérande. Allier,
France.

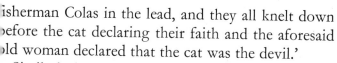

isherman Colas in the lead, and they all knelt down
before the cat declaring their faith and the aforesaid
old woman declared that the cat was the devil.'

Similarly in Brittany, Françoise Secrétain saw the
devil in 1598 'in the shape of a cat,' and Roland
Bernois testified 'that the devil appeared on the
sabbath in the shape of a large black cat. And all

those present went and kissed the black cat's behind.' In 1652 another witch confessed that 'the devil came to her room disguised as a cat, then changed into a man, dressed in red, who carried her off to the sabbath.'

In the countryside near Audierne (Brittany), we learn that the pacts were inscribed on the register belonging to 'the black cat, a favourite disguise of the devil.'

In Touraine, a cats' sabbath takes place during the night of Shrove Tuesday until dawn on Ash Wednesday, presided over by a 'large black cat, playing the violin.'

In the old province of Marche in France (covering today the *départements* of Creuse, Indre, Haute Vienne), the devil in the shape of a black cat was supposed to attend the dying, sitting on the bedhead waiting for the soul to take flight. An old woman of

Franche-Comté, suspected of having made a pact with the devil, lay on the point of death; a huge black cat sitting on the bed gazed steadfastly at the dying woman. The attendants tried in vain to chase it away; no sooner was it put out and the door closed firmly behind it than it reappeared in its place on the bed: 'It was the devil waiting to claim the old woman's soul.'

A pagan of antiquity would have seen it in a different light: for him the cat would be the guardian, the *Genius*, one of the shades watching over his protégé in order to continue protecting him in the next life.

As we have seen, it was the black cat that was supposed to be the devil. Black, white and red are the three fundamental colors of Christian symbolism. In natural symbolism, black signifies the absence of light, the invisible, the night. Hence everything connected with night, and especially evil, hell, the underworld, fertility, secret riches and, of course, the devil himself, were incorporated in the same symbol. For is not the devil evil personified? He inhabits the underworld-hell; and does he not make his own both fertile and rich? We shall see below how the Provençal 'Matagot' and the Breton 'Silver Cat' brought riches to their owners. They were black cats. And again it was in the shape of a black cat that the devil brought money to the 'father of a soothsayer from Cap-Sizun, who had had sexual relations with him!'

Perhaps for this reason the devil is called 'Old Moneybags' almost everywhere in France.

RITUAL WITCHCRAFT AND THE CAT

Popular traditions and witchcraft trials from all parts of Europe supply detailed descriptions of the ceremonies and magic rituals in which the cats played a part, starting with the pacts between a postulant

In many parts of France, the Devil was familiarly known as *Trainesac* ('Moneybags') because he was supposed to make people rich. Bibliothèque Nationale, Paris.

The cat was present at different kinds of magic ritual.

67

At ceremonies of magic incantation, the cat played an important role.

and the devil. Such pacts were quite common in Brittany and one example is related by Sébillot:

'You must catch a green frog at full moon and put it in an anthill, chanting all the time:

Fear not, frog, go make your way
To Satan's lair and beg him pray
To make me rich and send me gold
Then I'll not work when I am old.

'These preliminaries completed, you must go to a crossroads where five paths meet and at the stroke of twelve pronounce the following incantation:

Here at midnight I will wait,
To make a pact and seal my fate
Faithful to the end I'll be
Serving to eternity
Satan and his hideous brood
To the four corners of the world.

'At these words the devil will appear on one of the four roads, a black cat will come down the path opposite, a white hen on another, the green frog and an army of ants on the fourth. Only the fifth path remains, the one by which the postulant arrived at the crossroads. That one is reserved for his safe return once the conditions of the pact, hammered out in detail, have been accepted by both parties. One of the witnesses—cat, hen or frog—belongs by right to the person who has sold his soul, and will follow and remain to be his servitor. The cat is generally chosen for this role.'

So the cat becomes the Guardian Spirit of the initiate as we have already seen in Chapter IV.

Such pacts with the devil were not just popular stories. Some were actually drawn up, if we are to believe the accounts of the participants, and a good many came into the possession of the Inquisition. De Lancre mentions them in his writings. Originally contracts were drawn up and signed on parchment. Later they were said to be written in a book. Hence the Breton tale that they were inscribed 'in the Black Cat's register, which was the devil in disguise.' The applicant always signed with blood, usually drawn from his left arm. It will be remembered that at that time—quite beside the fact that ink was not easily come by in the countryside—blood made the contract a matter of life and death.

The pact could be for an unlimited time, or for a fixed number of years. Texts and tradition put the time between seven and nine years, recalling the pagan cycle of religious sacrifice that still existed in Gaul after the advent of Christianity.

Frazer describes the feast of Zeus, the Wolf-God celebrated every nine years in Arcady. A man ate the entrails of a human sacrifice, mixed with those of animals; he was thus transformed into a wolf, remaining in that shape for nine years. If he never touched human flesh during that time he became a man again. If he wanted to continue as a wolf the ritual had to be repeated. Moreover many Greek kings were allowed to reign only eight years and after that lapse of time they had to be reconsecrated. If they were

The cat seemingly
watches over this
child of the slums.
Octave Landuyt:
Slum Child.

When the pact had been signed, Satan placed his mark somewhere on the body; the silhouette of a cat can be made out in this one. Drawing by Claude Estang, after books of magic and the trial of Urbain Grandier.

incompetent they were replaced. Plutarch says the custom was carried out at intervals of nine years because when the Greeks calculated the time they included the waiting periods between them.

It was also at eight year intervals that the Athenians had to send seven young men and seven girls to Minos as a ritual sacrifice at the feast of renewal of the king's divine power. The same period determined the year of the cyclical Coronation Feast at Delphi and the Feast of the Laurel at Thebes, which celebrated a god-hero killing a dragon.

Frazer believed that the eight-year cycle was based on exact astronomical observations; although the sun and the moon come into conjunction once a month, it is a fact that they always meet at a different point in the heavens. About eight years must elapse before the paths of the two stars cross in the same part of the sky. Furthermore the full moon coincides with either the shortest or the longest day only once every eight years.

So it is not surprising that the deposition or ritual death of the king-priest-god coincided with the end of an astronomical cycle. When the sun and moon had run their course and a new cycle began, it followed that the king had to renew his divinity or prove it to be unimpaired in competition with a more vigorous successor.

It is therefore conceivable that the length of time the devil allowed sorcerers and witches, varying between seven and nine years, could mean that they, too, had become substitutes for the royal or divine victim. Witnesses at witchcraft trials attested that the devil promised power and riches to the initiate for a fixed period of years. When it was over, he had to render up body and soul to the devil. After the contract was signed Satan made a mark somewhere on the body of his new follower. It was usually a blue or red imprint of a cat's paw.

These marks were the first thing the inquisitor looked for when a woman suspected of witchcraft fell into his hands. If the mark was not plain to see then he assumed it must be hidden in the secret parts, on the membranes. The witch was shaven and examined all over. The mark itself was supposed to be insensitive. So the accused was stabbed all over with long needles until it was discovered: the wound should not bleed, nor must the witch scream. Discovery of the mark was definite proof of guilt. So the inquisitor simply went on until the woman stopped screaming. Was it because the 'insensitive spot' had been found or because the wretched creature was too weak to cry out after such torture? The most famous specialists, Springer, Delrio, Boguet, Bodin and de Lancre left awe-inspiring accounts of the trials they presided over, full of the horrendous details of the torture inflicted on the accused. The inquisitorial zeal of these judges often came very near to sadism. One even went so far as to boast that his justice 'was so excellent' that the accused killed themselves to escape: and Bodin relates that even the smallest of the 'detestable crimes' of which a witch is accused deserves, as he says, 'an exquisite death.'

The mark was generally given to the new adept during a sabbath. The dictionary definition of sabbath is 'a nocturnal, noisy assembly of sorcerers and witches.' Nobody, however, explains why the word is supposed to derive from the Hebrew *shabbath* which means rest. The witches' sabbath has nothing to do with rest. It is, on the contrary, a gathering for the ceremony of initiation: dances opening and closing the séance; feasting, orgiastic ritual, and sacrifice and prayers resembling the homage paid to a god.

It would make better sense if the word were derived from the Greek *Sabazia*. Phrygian bacchanalia were so-called because Bacchus was called Sabazios in that country. Demosthenes gives a vivid description of the cult in his discourse against Eschine. The witches' sabbath seems far closer to th

The most famous
inquisitors left
gruesome records
of the trials of
witches, describing
in detail the tortures
inflicted on the
accused.
Zentralbibliothek,
Zurich: Ms. F 26,
fol. 227r.

antique bacchanalia than to the Hebrew day of rest. The Sabazios were indeed turbulent assemblies, orgies of dancing and screaming in homage to a fertility god. Legends and stories describe the same kind of activity at a Cats' sabbath.

In the province of Maine in France the cats congregate at crossroads in lonely places, sometimes very near large rocks where they make their presence felt by miaowing. Only cats at least eight years old can take part, and one cat is killed at every meeting.

In Poitou the cats on their way to the sabbath follow the road from the church of Saint-Laurent at Montcoutant and gather at l'Ormeau-Robinet, better known as 'Timbre aux Chats' because they used to drink there from a granite trough. The sound of their cries and crunching jaws could be heard all night, as well as 'the sharpening of their terrible claws ready for anyone who comes to disturb their feasting.'

In Ile-de-France people thought that cats gathered for a grisly sabbath on St. John's Eve. In Touraine, Berry and the central provinces of France, the cats' sabbath took place on the night of Shrove Tuesday until dawn on Ash Wednesday. The meetings were usually held at the foot of a cross or at a crossroads. Likewise in the Ille-et-Vilaine *département* on carnival night, the cats held their sabbath beside a rock called 'The Sorcerer's Chamber,' in an orchard near Montfort.

Margaret Murray's view is that the sacrifice of an eight-year-old animal at every meeting equates the cat with the divine victim who was sacrificed in early pre-Christian religions, periods of seven, eight or

On the way to the sabbath. Goya: *¿Dónde va mamà?* The Warburg Institute, London.

The cat attends on the preparation of witches for the sabbath. Hans Baldung-Grien: *Hexenszene.* Albertina, Vienna.

nine years, depending on the regions. This sacrifice had a definite purpose: the sacrificial man, or later the symbolic animal, made the land fertile. Some authors have gone out of their way to describe the more or less imaginary horrors of the sabbath. Nothing was too exaggerated if it prevented the inquisitive from going to see what really happened, because Christianity was always struggling against the danger of a lapse into paganism.

The sabbath was, indeed, a pagan assembly, the crowds of worshippers being drawn from the people, although the leaders were aristocratic and occasionally even priests. We have already seen, for example, that the Bishop of Coventry was arraigned before the Pope for adhering to the old religion and worshipping the devil in the shape of a cat or a sheep.

The rites of the old pagan religion demonstrate, as far as we can tell from the witchcraft trials, that it was essentially a fertility cult, which explains the importance of orgies, wild and violent dancing and the sexual acts that followed. The aim of all these festivities was to increase the fertility of the land, for that was the main preoccupation of the worshippers who were nearly all peasants and farmers. The darkness brooding over places where sabbaths were held stresses the cult of the earth and the powers of the underworld, the source of the hidden riches every human longed to possess.

VI THE CAT IN TRADITIONAL FIRE CEREMONIES

The popular fire festivals of Europe, wherever and on whatever day they took place, had many things in common. The custom of lighting ceremonial fires, leaping over the flames, leading animals round the blaze or forcing them through the smoke is to be found in many countries, likewise the habit of organizing processions or torch races across fields, gardens, meadows and byres.

The fires were usually kindled in spring or summer. But some regions also lit them in late autumn and in winter, on Hallowe'en, Christmas Day and the Eve of Epiphany. In Europe the ritual burning of cats took place generally on the first Sunday in Lent and the feast of St. John. Incredible as it may seem this practice continued right up into the 20th century.

There are two interpretations of these fire festivals. Wilhelm Mannhardt believes that they were fertility rites whereas other authorities describe them as purification rites. In fact they complement each other. Fire is both a purification and a fertility symbol.

THE LENTEN FIRES

The first Sunday in Lent was usually called *Le Dimanche des Brandons* in France, because on that day people carried flaming torches, touching the branches of trees and the earth in their fields to make them fertile. The name varies from place to place. In northern France it was called *Le Dimanche du Béhour (or Béhourdi)*, from a local dialect word *behen* meaning 'a perch'. In Burgundy it was called *Le Dimanche des Bordes*. In Franche-Comté, *Le Dimanche des Piquérès* and in Bresse *Le Dimanche des Epicrées*.

However, the custom of lighting bonfires on the first Sunday in Lent was apparently the finale of the Carnival celebrations, because originally the *Brandon* was the same as the log fire used to burn the Carnival masks. That explains why it was sometimes held on Ash Wednesday. Cats were often burned in these fires.

In Picardy, for example, a pole called 'the perch' of the *Béhourdi* was erected in the village square, and baskets filled with cats placed around it. The people then set fire to the logs gathered at the foot of the pole. As the flames began to lick the willow cages, the lids were opened to release the wretched beasts that could only escape by climbing the pole. But they were overcome by the smoke almost at once, and fell back into the fire where they were burned alive.

In Burgundy, near Sémur-en-Auxois, on the *Dimanche des Bordes* a cat was tied to the end of a pole and children carried it round begging for firewood. Then they stuck the pole and the cat into the fire, and the poor creature was burned to death. Meanwhile the shepherds forced their animals through the flames and smoke to ward off sickness. When the cats had been burned, everyone lit torches from the dying embers and went off into orchards, fields and gardens, shaking the sparks of their torches over the cultivated ground; they carried them under the fruit trees, or shook some ash into the hens' nests. When all the ceremonies were over, they went home to feast.

Applying the flame to trees, fields, gardens and hens' nests was fertility magic.

ST. JOHN'S EVE FIRES

Bonfires were most common during the summer solstice on the Eve and the Day of St. John, June 24th. The pretence that this ritual was held in honor of John the Baptist gave it a superficial Christian aura, but its origin was undoubtedly much earlier. At the summer solstice the sun is at its highest and it is most unlikely that man would have allowed the day when the Life-Giver, the Destroyer of Evil Spirits, the Sun, reached its zenith to pass unnoticed.

The custom of kindling bonfires on St. John's Eve was so widespread in France that almost every town or village built one until about the middle of the 19th century. It was certainly a pagan custom to start with, but the Catholic Church pretended it was Christian by declaring outright that the fires celebrated the birth of John the Baptist, who happened, very conveniently, to have been born at the summer solstice, just as Christ's birthday falls in midwinter. It is strange that the Feast of St. John should be the only one to be celebrated with the same signal honor as that reserved by the Church for the Birth of Christ.

Jacques Bénigne Bossuet, the famous French seventeenth-century preacher and writer, explicitly confirms this edifying theory about the St. John fires. He told his catechumens that the Church itself took part in these illuminations because many parishioners not only in his own diocese of Meaux but in several others too, lit 'Ecclesiastical Fires' in the hope of suppressing the superstitions surrounding the usual bonfires. The superstitions he described were: 'Dancing round the fire, playing, feasting and singing improper songs; throwing plants into the

PORTRAIT DV MAGNIFIQVE BASTIMENT DE LA MAISON DE VILLE·DE PARIS·

blaze, picking them either fasting, or before noon, then bringing them home and keeping them for a year; preserving the firebrands or wood ash and other like things.'

Strabo, the Greek geographer, is often quoted as having said that the Celts practised holocaust: they used to burn condemned men in huge osier cages. As time passed, human victims were gradually replaced by animals, but the animals still had to have some symbolic value in their eyes, and it is interesting to note that the sacrificial animals were nearly always cats.

During the St. John fires held in the Place de Grève in Paris, they burned a basket, barrel or sack full of live cats suspended from a pole above the fire. The Parisians gathered the ash and the charred wood and took it home, convinced that it would bring good luck.

Kings of France were often present at these festivities and sometimes lit the fire. In 1648,

It was customary to burn a basket or sack full of live cats on the St. John's Eve bonfire erected in the Place de Grève, Paris. Engraving by Mérian, 1645.

77

Louis XIV, wearing a crown of roses, with a bunch of roses in his hand, kindled the fire, danced and attended the banquet that followed in the townhall. But that was the last time a king presided over the St. John's Eve fires in Paris.

Jacques Antoine Dulaure (1755–1835), the historian, described one of these events from the reign of Charles IX (1550–74): 'A sixty-foot tree was erected in the Place de Grève, with wooden crossbars, to which five hundred kindling faggots and two hundred bundles of medium-sized firewood were fixed. The foot was then stacked round with ten cartloads of large logs (about seventy cubic feet) and a lot of straw. One hundred and twenty town archers and a hundred men with harquebuses were present to control the crowds; also musicians, the so-called "great band", seven resounding trumpeters, all added to the splendid noise. The civil officers, merchant-provosts and municipal magistrates carrying yellow wax torches, advanced towards the heap of logs and kindling around the tree and presented King Charles with a white wax torch, embellished with two red velvet handles. The king solemnly carried the torch and set light to the fire.'

At the top of the tree hung a barrel or sack of live cats, as shown by the Register of Paris: 'Paid to Lucas Pommerieux, a guard on the embankment, 100 Paris sous, for supplying, over a period of years ending at Saint-Jean 1573, all the cats required for the customary fire and for supplying a large canvas sack to contain the said cats.'

Allusion to the cats of St. John was made at the time of the Catholic League in the 14th century by a lampoonist, who disposes of Henri of Navarre (the future Henri IV) and his followers in the following manner: 'They ought to arrest them on St. John's Eve as a sacrifice to St. John. If they slung them from the wood of the tall tree, putting the king in the barrel where they stick the cats, it would make a worthy sacrifice to heaven and a pleasing spectacle for the whole country.'

They burned cats on St. John's Eve almost everywhere in France not only in Paris but from the Alps to Brittany, where the custom persisted until the Revolution. In Lyonnais, at Feurs, Dance and Saint-Bernard-des-Cars, it was insulting to call someone a cat. The inhabitants of Saint-Chamond were nicknamed, *Couramiauds* because on St. John's Eve they used to chase after *(courir)* a scorched and terrified cat that had managed to escape from the fire into which they had thrown it.

R. de Westphalen describes a festival still held at Metz in the 18th century with great pomp:

'The Chief Magistrate, wearing the uniform and insignia of his rank, accompanied by the advisory magistrate, by the deputies of the three orders, by the Major and his assistant of the civil militia, by town sergeants and six halberdiers, went first to the Town Hall in Haute-Pierre, where they were received by the Governor with much fanfare and the sound of the cannon in the square. The procession started with music by the town garrison. After the Swiss Guard came the Governor's private guard, the six halberdiers of the Chief Magistrate and two town sergeants bearing a white wax torch. Behind in the same procession walked the Governor and the Chief Magistrate, followed by civil and military authorities. When they reached the esplanade the two magistrates walked three times around the bonfire which had thirteen cats imprisoned in a wooden cage on the top; they took the white wax torches from the Town Major and another Officer, and set light to the fire. The flames licked and burned the cage until the half-burned cats either fell onto the fire or escaped. All the time the people screamed 'Noel', and danced in a ring singing the round of St. John. In the end, the wife of the Maréchal of Armentières interceded, and after 1777 the animals were no longer sacrificed.'

The bonfires of Metz depicted by a contemporary artist. Drawing by Jean Morette, Batilly.

Tessier, *sous-préfet* of Thionville and a contributor to the Société des Antiquaires, wrote in 1822: 'I was present once more at the ceremonial St. John bonfire at Metz; less than sixty years ago a dozen cats were burned in wicker cages for the amusement of the populace.'

Elsewhere, in the province of Meurthe for example, the custom of burning cats did not die out until 1905! Less frequently cats were burned on Christmas Eve in bonfires that marked the winter solstice. Traces still remain in the *Landes*, the pine-covered region in Gascony, where the villagers used to set off at dusk for the fields carrying a straw torch fastened to a stake and singing:

Halhe Nadau	(Christmas Bonfire
Lou trip ou pan	Throw the sausage on the floor
Lou gat ou hum	The cat on the fire
Pum!	Pum!)

The torches were kindled at the Christmas bonfire where a cat fastened to a stake was being roasted.

These examples demonstrate that the traditional bonfires were ceremonial rites in which everyone participated.

The February bonfires held at the end of winter after Carnival would therefore have originally been fertility rites. Carnival, of course, used to begin at the Feast of the Three Kings—the season when the

79

Shades come to visit the living, bringing fertility, health and abundance, and driving evil influences away. The Celts called the dead 'The Strong Ones,' and archaic thought held that physical life depended on periodic renewal of contact with the Beyond. The heads of many early Carnival masks are made of cats' skins, not only in the north, in Germany and Austria, where such masks are common, but also in several parts of France, where Carnival hats are decorated with cats' skins.

So the spring bonfires were intended to propitiate the powers of the Other World and to cause the corn, buried in the ground all winter, to germinate in due time. Burning the cat in the fire was a symbolic destruction of witches and, at the same time, was believed to destroy the evil influences preventing fertility.

The Fires of St. John played a double role of purification and fertilization. At the season the corn was already growing, so it was a question of protecting it from potential enemies. Of these, evil spirits were the worst because their spells could prevent the corn from ripening or cause storms to destroy the crops. Even worse, they could bring disease to man and beast—which was why all the people and the animals as well had to jump over the St. John fires when the flames died down. Girls who found a spark in their skirt would be married within the year: the power of the flame made them fertile and protected them against spells.

We have seen how the cat was commonly thought to be the incarnation of a witch from the Middle Ages until today, and that they burned cats in the fires of St. John because they thought they were in this way destroying witches and purifying. They no longer sacrified to germinate the corn, but tried to protect it, and bring in as rich a harvest as possible, and in the same way they tried to protect their animals by forcing them to jump over the fire. Cremation of the cat was a transferred extermination

During Carnival
time the spirits of
the dead visit the
living world. James
Ensor: *Carnival*.
Stedelijk Museum,
Amsterdam.

On St John's Eve, cats were burned to protect the coming harvest against evil spirits and witches. Brueghel the Elder: *Les Feux de la Saint-Jean*.

of witches, who could not be burned in the flesh because they could not be unmasked.

In its fight against paganism, the Church took over the rites that it failed to suppress; secular tradition cannot be changed overnight. The pagan, ritual bonfires were described as purifying fires aimed at man's enemies; townspeople and villagers were neither alienated nor deprived of their entertainment and were converted.

After its veneration in Egypt and recognition as a Guardian Spirit in the classical world, cats suffered from a reaction lasting nearly 1,500 years, caused by a change of religion. They suffered the same fate as the Druidesses, who were called witches. One of the most famous of the nine Druidesses from the island of Sein off the Brittany coast, was called Catta. They were crowned with verbena, a sacred plant, one of sixteen midsummer flowers gathered on St. John's Eve to make crosses and crowns. Nor must we forget that every symbol is two-sided: a Sun-Hero has also his dark self, his contact with the Underworld and with fertility.

In Greece the entrance to the underworld was called 'The Door of the Sun.' The polarity of light and dark, solar and chthonic, shows the two faces of a single reality.

His skill as a ratter saved the cat from extinction during the witch-hunts. Bosch: *Le Jardin a Délices*. Prado, Madrid.

VII THE DOMESTIC CAT FROM THE MIDDLE AGES TO THE PRESENT DAY

The cat, unlike other domestic animals, has never been limited in its activity. Dogs guard and hunt, the horse is a means of transport, but although the cat is undoubtedly a rat-catcher—it was no doubt this that helped him to survive the apalling witch-hunts and mass burnings—he nevertheless has a completely different side to his character. His magnetic personality and secret affinity with women reserve a special place for him in the family home. A few examples will soon demonstrate how the cat's flexible nature influenced different human attitudes.

GUARDIAN SPIRIT

In the 14th century, a poor young man called Richard Whittington decided to seek his fortune in India. He found a ship willing to take him and his only possession—a cat. A storm arose in the Indian Ocean wrecking the ship on an unknown shore. The whole crew was taken prisoner by the natives and brought before their king. During the royal audience Whittington noticed that the place was infested with rats and mice which scampered about, even around the king's throne. The young Englishman let loose his cat which killed and scattered the rodents. The king was delighted to be delivered from the scourge, and expressed his gratitude by making Whittington his favourite, and dubbing the cat General of his armies. He had, in fact, no other enemies. For years Whittington was the most important person in the kingdom. One day he longed to go home to England; the king agreed, provided he left the cat. In exchange he was given a ship laden with riches. When he reached London he was elected Lord Mayor, and to show that he owed it all to his cat, he took its name and was known henceforward as 'Milord Cat.' He became one of the richest and important men in the country. He was the founder of many public buildings, one of which is now the Stock Exchange.

Not only witches were accompanied by their domestic familiar; this portrait of the Count of Southampton by John de Critz shows the importance acquired by the cat.

There is an engraving in existence showing him stroking the cat, and one can still see a statue of Whittington's cat on Highgate Hill in London.

There are several versions of this story, although it is based on an authentic record. Some locate the shipwreck in Africa, not India. But one fact remains constant throughout: Whittington owed his fame to his cat. It was his Guardian Spirit.

It was customary, as we have said, to inject a few drops of the blood of a sacred cat into the arm of a child dedicated to Bastet. This practice appears again in sixteenth-century England where witches were always accompanied by their 'familiar' (animal attached to their persons), often represented in the shape of a cat.

In 1579, Mother Dowell, a notorious witch of Windsor, kept a spirit embodied in a cat called Giles, which always attended her séances. She fed it on milk mixed with drops of her own blood. This

offering was intended to ensure the animal's protection.

It is a remarkable fact that traditions can exist and have the same significance although they are geographically far apart. The Egyptians believed that Bastet protected men against contagious disease: the same belief is found in Lorraine. In fact anyone owning a three-coloured cat (the russet colour is essential) need have no fear of fever.

In the fifteenth-century cathedral of St. Omer is a statue of the seated Virgin suckling the infant Jesus. The heads of the ox and the ass can be seen at the

Anybody with a tortoiseshell cat (the red is important), is safe from fevers, as a Lorraine proverb has it.

The statue of Dick Whittington still stands on Highgate Hill, London.

The medieval sculptor did not hesitate to place the Virgin and Child under the protection of the *Cat-Genius*. Cathedral of Saint-Omer, Pas-de-Calais, France.

aware of the animal's role, and that he was placing the Mother and Child under its protection.

So the cat preserved its protective character throughout the ages. It reappears in this story from Franche-Comté: at Luze, a village near Mont Vaudois, there was talk of 'strange happenings in the night.' One young woman said: 'I will go up the mountain and I am sure nothing will happen.' She left with a cat in her apron. When she got to the top she cried: 'Here I am at the top of Mount Vaudois.' A voice replied: 'If you hadn't brought your cat you

Artists have always kept alive the cat's role of Guardian Angel of the new-born infant. Jacopo Zucchi: *Birth of St John*. Church of San Giovanni Decollato, Rome.

back of the niche and a cat crouches at the Virgin's feet. We have already noticed the cat set at the feet of the statue of Liberty in Rome, and it can be seen in the same position in allegories illustrating the political theories of the French Revolution. This humble position typifies the animal's habitual reserve. That does not make its protection any less effective however. To find it here beside the Virgin and Child seems to prove that the medieval artist was well

Birth of Saint-Rémi, with the cat among those present. Detail of a tapestry. Musée des Beaux-Arts, Rheims.

Women in
particular have
always loved the
cat, from the Middle
Ages to the present
day. *Les Très*

*Riches Heures du
Duc de Berry,* Musée
Condé, Chantilly;
P. Bonnard, *La
Dame au Chat,*
Kunsthalle, Bremen.

In the humblest of
homes the cat
occupies a favored
place. J.-J. de
Boissieu: *La Veillée.*
Bibliothèque
Nationale, Paris.

would never have got away from here.' She was in a
terrible state when she came down. But she was
proved right: she got home safe and sound, thanks,
she thought, to her cat.

As a guardian, the cat had certain rights. In France
and Belgium it was so much part of the family that
they hung a little black ribbon round its neck when

someone died in the house. In many provinces it was
the custom to hang a piece of black crepe on the
beehives because bees also were guardians of the
hearth. We have already seen the cat in this role in
Rome and in Roman Gaul. In medieval France it was
called the 'House Cat' and when a new cat came into
the house it occasioned a special ritual: 'Whoever

88

The cat watches
over the whole
family. Rembrandt:
*Le Ménage du
Menuisier*. Musée
du Louvre.

By the seventeenth century, the cat had become a pet in even bourgeois homes. Van Veen: *Le Peintre et sa Famille*. Musée du Louvre.

would keep his cat at home without straying has to take the cat and carry it three times round the pot-hanger and then rub its paws against the wall of the chimney, and if it is properly done, the cat will never leave.'

These fifteenth-century customs have not completely vanished. A similar tradition was still customary in Liège in the early 20th century. 'Rub a new cat's paws with butter and carry it three times round the pot-hanger, then make it sharpen its claws on the outside of the chimney.' In Gironde it

has to walk in the form of a cross. In Lorraine they also hang a bunch of dried savory over the door. Some other regions carried the cat in a sack seven times around the pot-hanger, but in Germany three times was enough.

The adult cat became so much part of the family that it was never on any account allowed to be carried far away from the house for fear of some calamity. The only safe way to move the animal was to repeat the ritual performed when it arrived. Another bad omen was for a cat to die under its master's roof:

91

for this to happen was a sure sign of impending doom.

The desire to enjoy the cat's protection also gave rise to a barbaric custom: a live cat would be bricked into the façade when a house was being built. Monseigneur Barbier de Montault witnessed it in Vienne in 1849 when a house owned by a country gentleman called de la Perrière, near Loudun, was being reconstructed. The custom was fairly widespread in France, and, on occasions, skeletons of cats come to light when old houses are being demolished.

In his *Mémoires d'outre-tombe*, Chateaubriand, describing life in his château de Combourg in Brittany, says that people believed that the ghost of one of the counts of Combourg, who had lived three hundred years before and who had a wooden leg, used to walk from time to time and that someone had met him on the great staircase of the tower. His wooden leg could occasionally be seen walking alone followed by a black cat. These tales were explained when the castle was being restored in 1876, for on a fifteenth-century beam they found the skeleton of a cat, perfectly preserved.

As late as the 19th century in Denmark, peasants of Jutland used to bury a live cat at the threshold of their cottages. The dead animal became the guardian of the house. When Laura died, Petrarch took her cat; on its death, he had it embalmed in the Egyptian manner and placed it over his doorway, thus perpetuating its protective role.

The habit of immuring a live cat in a façade, under a roof or doorstep appears a gratuitous barbarism today. The tradition does show, however, the belief in animals' souls, some of which, like that of the cat, were beneficent. Christianity denied that any animal had a soul and in the Middle Ages even excluded women! But the earliest historical beliefs died hard. Sorceresses kept them alive and for a long time their atavistic preference for cats had a baleful influence on the wretched beasts. The Middle Ages did not, however, get rid of the contradictions entirely: while burning cats in the St. John bonfires, they still placed the tutelary cat on the arms of cities of Normandy and Poitou and it also appeared on the escutcheons of a hundred or so European families.

DEATH AND THE CAT

The cat, so closely associated with the house and family, has sometimes been seen as a herald of death. The warning signs are unmistakable. In the Baltic lands, in Germany, Italy, Belgium and France, if a cat jumps onto the bed of a sick person, their end is near. Sometimes it is exactly the opposite: a cat accustomed to sleep on its master's bed, will leave if the person is dying.

A cat can also foretell death from a distance. One night a Breton farmer from Dol set off to visit his neighbour, Burlotte. As he was walking along a lonely road bordered with oak trees he saw the eyes

To ensure prosperity, builders walled up living cats in the façades of houses. Drawing of a skeleton found during a demolition by Claude Estang.

The Romantic writer Chateaubriand recounts a legend of the Comte de Combourg whose ghost haunted a staircase in the tower of his castle (opposite). Sometimes his wooden leg was to be seen walking alone, accompanied by a black cat.

f three cats shining down at him from the branches f an apple tree. Through their miaowing he distin-uished a voice speaking to him: 'Hurry, my good ellow, hurry to the village and tell them that Bur-otte is dead.' He hurried to his neighbour's house nly to find her dead.

NATURAL DEATH OF A CAT

When they sense that they are dying, animals gener-ally—and this includes the cat—go away from home. So it might seem an ill omen either for the house or one of the family if a cat dies in its own home. But

Arms of Chaffardon, Normandy.

king's experience. In an attempt to gain the confidence and collaboration of the natives, whom he knew to be cat-worshippers, the Colonel ordered white cats to be painted on the army vehicles as well as at various points along the planned path of the road he wanted to construct. The air force was also instructed to collect as many white cats as possible for their camp. The natives assumed that the sacred cats had come to the aerodrome of their own accord and concluded that the gods were on the Allies' side. So they thought it best to side with them and ignore Japanese propaganda.

The explanation for this lay in the Burmese religious feelings towards the cat. They believe that the animal watches over their well-being, and is a divine dispenser of truth, and they therefore treat it like an oracle to be obeyed without question.

The story of Titichane describes how the killing of a cat brought disaster to a whole tribe. The same fatalistic attitude is found in the Arab world where no one would dare to hurt a cat. The Black Africans brought similar ideas to America.

In many European countries, the belief is that it is tempting providence to ill-treat a cat, and to kill one intentionally will result in certain death.

In tenth-century Wales, Howel the Good made a law which shows us the value they put on the domestic cat. The price of a cat is recorded, and also the scale of punishment meted out to anyone who tortured, wounded or killed one. As well as corporal punishment the delinquent had to give, as an indemnity, a ewe with her lamb, or alternatively, supply enough corn to cover the corpse of the cat as it hung by its tail with the muzzle touching the ground.

The Madagascar code has similar laws: a cat thief is imprisoned for a fortnight, but if he returns it, for five days only. No allusion is made to killing a cat, perhaps because no Madagascan would dare to commit such a crime, knowing full well that his own death would immediately follow.

it must be remembered that the cat is also the Guardian Spirit of the house and its inhabitants.

Expressions of mourning in Europe never reached the height attained by the Egyptians for their cats. Nevertheless, although they are less eloquent, they still show the high regard reserved for the animal and the undiminished fear caused by the cat's death in the house. In France, Belgium, and Germany it is a portent of great misfortune.

CONSEQUENCES FOLLOWING
THE KILLING OF A CAT

We have already described the frenzy that seized the Egyptians when a cat died, and the use the Persian king Cambyses made of it. During the last war, an English Officer in Burma made use of the Persian

94

THE CAT AS A SOURCE OF RICHES

Since the cat was the guardian spirit of the individual,
his family, house and sustenance, it is natural that
its role should be extended to that other aspect of
man's aspirations—wealth. This idea is illustrated in
the best known story of all—Puss-in-Boots, the tale
of a poor boy becoming rich with the aid of his
magic cat. In Africa alone we find ten different versions of this tale. Its theme is also found in other
stories, such as this Tuscan fairy tale: 'One day a
poor woman with many children met a fairy, who
told her to climb to the top of the mountain nearby
where she would find a beautiful palace inhabited by

enchanted cats, who would put an end to her poverty. The woman went up and a small cat let her in without saying a word; he knew why she had come. Then he invited her to do some small tasks for the inhabitants of the castle. The woman agreed and swept the rooms, lit the fires, washed up, drew water from the well, made the beds and baked bread for the cats. When all was complete she was brought before the king of the cats. He received her seated on a golden throne with a golden crown on his head. She curtsied to him and asked for help. The king pulled a golden chain to ring a little bell to assemble all the cats. They told him that the woman had done her work well. Then he commanded them to fill her apron with gold coins before leaving the castle. She returned home and her sister, seeing such a fortune, decided to go to visit the cats herself, but instead of helping them with their tasks she mistreated them. She came home scratched, frightened to death and, of course, empty-handed.'

Everywhere in Europe the cat is believed to bring wealth. The Swedish-Estonian *skrate* and the *bjära* of the Finno-Swedes was a goblin in the form of a cat who brought good fortune and wealth to a house. In return for his favor, he had to be given a part of everything there was and if ever this was refused him, he left the house and offered his magic services elsewhere.

In Germany the house-sprite, also in the shape of a cat, is commanded by his master to find and bring home good fortune and riches as well as milk, corn, meat and every kind of food.

The same superstition can be found in all the French provinces. In the south and south-west, people often talk of the *Matagot*. He is supposed to take the shape of a cat, usually black, and lives in the house 'like a kind of household god.' He brings his owner good luck on condition that he is well provided for. He lives on bouillon, meat and 'everything of the best from the table': *se dona al Matagot la pri-*

96

This tenth-century Welsh law evidences the high status accorded to the cat in Wales.

The Laws of Howel the Good, Prince of South Wales

The worth of a cat and her tiethi (qualities) is this:

1. The worth of a kitten from the night it is kittened until it shall open its eyes is a legal penny.

2. And from that time, until it shall kill mice, two legal pence.

3. And after it shall kill mice, four legal pence; and so it always remains.

4. Her tiethi are, to see, to hear, to kill mice, to have her claws entire, to rear and not devour her kittens, and if she be bought, and be deficient in any one of these tiethi; let one third of her worth be returned.

Of Cats:

1. The worth of a cat that is killed or stolen: its head to be put downwards upon a clean even floor, with its tail lifted upwards, and thus suspended, whilst wheat is poured about it, until the tip of its tail be covered; and that is to be its worth; if the corn cannot be had a milch sheep, with her lamb and her wool, is its value; if it be a cat which guards the King's barn.

2. The worth of a common cat is four legal pence.

3. Whoever shall sell a cat is to answer for her not going a caterwauling every moon; and that she devour not her kittens; and that she have ears, eyes, teeth and nails; and being a good mouser.

Puss-in-Boots,
bringer of riches
and good fortune
to his master, by

Moritz von
Schwind: *Der
gestiefelte Kater*.

mera bocada (the *Matagot* must have the first mouthful). Mistral wrote about them in his *Mémoires*: 'There were black cats called *Matagots* which brought money to the houses where they lived... you remember, surely, old Mother Tartavelle, who left so much money when she died? Well, she had a black cat and at every meal she threw the first mouthful under the table to him.' In Rome the first mouthful was likewise offered to the household god. By this means the *Matagot*'s owner found an *écu* in his coffer or a few gold *louis* in his slipper every morning.

In Lyonnais they think the black cat is lucky as long as it has a small white tuft in the coat, and that if you find a piece of his dung in your shoe you will soon be sure to get money.

If you are lucky you may meet Fairy Gouttière, the name given to a strange cat which gives a bottomless purse to those who please him. In Lorraine a man who makes a quick fortune is said to 'have a black cat.'

In Brittany, where tradition dies harder than anywhere else, it is considered unlucky to kill a cat, because cats bring wealth to their protectors. The most elaborate versions of the 'Legend of the Silver Cat' are Breton. If someone becomes rich overnight without a satisfactory explanation for the origin of their sudden fortune, they are said to have found the 'Silver Cat.' This 'Silver Cat' is always a much cherished black cat. If its owners wanted the cat to go and look for money, before they went to bed they put a purse beside him, one side full of gold, the other empty, and then commanded him to go and do his duty. As soon as the light was extinguished, the cat went out carrying the purse, and one could be sure he would return the next morning, or soon after, with twice the amount of money in the purse. To repeat the performance, it was essential not to replace any of the money used the first time, because coins were no good a second time.

Another version has it that the woman of the house offer her breast and suckle the cat on the eve of its departure to find money. On its return, because the cat is exhausted, they must have ready 'a bowl of soup and the housewife must warm his feet and belly before the fire, caressing him with gentle hands.'

The theme is constant: the cat is treated as a kind of god who must be honored and respected to make him use his power to help you and to dispense happiness and good fortune. He is still in the role of 'spirit,' protector both of the individual and the house, because he always brings the treasure home.

In all these legends and beliefs the materialization of riches means gold. Even the 'Silver Cat' brings gold coins and the word silver in this case is abstract and synonymous with good luck.

The *Matagot* in the shape of a black cat brings his owner good fortune—so long as he is well fed.

The cats all bring gold in payment for care or a service rendered. Sometimes, as in the Tuscan fairy tale, their grandeur is such that they live surrounded by golden objects. They are the direct descendants of Bastet, daughter of the Sun-God, who is often depicted with a gold ring in her ear. From the earliest times, gold was the metal symbolizing the sun, and in ancient Egypt it was thought to be the embodiment of Râ

LOVE AND THE CAT

The cat is a voluptuous animal and loves being stroked. Its nocturnal prowlings have turned it into a purely carnal symbol as well as one of love. This is another example of the ambivalent attitude evoked by the cat—sacred versus profane love.

Throughout northern Europe and Germany, marriages often took place on a Friday—Freya's day. Goddess of Love, Freya watched over human marriages and ensured their fecundity. If the sun shone during the ceremony the bride was said 'to have fed the cat well'—which meant that she would be a good housekeeper.

In Flanders they claimed that a girl who fondled a cat in the hopes of finding a handsome husband was sure to marry one. Girls in Lorraine and Franche-Comté cherished the same hope if they loved cats, and in Poitou if they treated them well.

In Transylvania, a month after a wedding, the people brought a cat in a cradle to the house of the newly-weds and rocked the cradle in their presence to ensure fine children. Perhaps Albrecht Dürer had the same idea when he put a huge cat in the foreground with Adam and Eve at the foot of the Tree of Life. It has been suggested that it was under that tree that Adam and Eve conceived Abel.

Hurting a cat intentionally during the wedding ceremony was an attempt to suppress the tutelary power of the animal and therefore to harm his protégés. In east Prussia envious malefactors tied two cats together by the tail, and forced them to cross the path of the wedding procession, a sign of ill-omen for the newly married couple.

Even involuntary clumsiness is a bad augury. In the 15th century it was believed that the way you treated a cat influenced love affairs. The following extract from the *Evangile des Quenouilles* is interesting: 'No young person should dislike a cat, because they bring good fortune, making a girl lucky in love and

In northern Europe, Freya, goddess of love, chose the cat as her symbol. Cathedral of Schleswig.

The Diable d' Argent (the Money-Devil) brought wealth disguised as a black cat, called *Le Chat d' Argent* (the Money-Cat). Bibliothèque Nationale, Paris.

A custom that goes back way into the dawn of history is that of pulling 'Moneybags' or the *Diable d' Argent* by the tail. Bibliothèque Nationale, Paris.

ensuring that she grows into a beautiful and gracious lady.' Even in the 20th century, any girl from Lyonnais or Lorraine who carelessly treads on a cat's tail delays her wedding for a year. At Quimper she will look in vain for a bridegroom for seven years.

Negligence also brings bad luck: in Flanders if a cat sits by the door just before a wedding, the young couple will have bad luck; the animal is thus reproaching the young bride for not looking after him properly.

The cat is also used metaphorically in the language of love. If a Breton girl refuses a young man's hand in marriage, she is said to have 'given him the cat.' In south-eastern Belgium this idea is even more marked: the young girl hands her unfortunate suitor a cat and tells him 'to count the hairs.' This reply is considered to be a gross insult as well as a rebuff. The same offensive language is used for a husband who lets his wife beat him. Things are a little different in Burgundy: the villagers assemble noisily in front of the feeble husband's house and throw a cat from one to the other, hurting it all the time. This they call 'doing the cat'; they are symbolically attacking the *Genius Loci* of an unhappy home.

Weddings have been celebrated with rejoicing throughout the ages, but second marriages are different. Widows who remarried laid themselves open to mockery. In ancient Egypt, Arabia and southern Germany, a cat was hung outside their window as a sign of disapproval. The cat symbolized the excess of sensuality, true cause of the new union as it was thought. In Gascony, near Dax, a second marriage aroused particularly violent displays. The people surrounded the couple's house carrying torches and singing scurrilous songs composed for the occasion. The whole crowd demanded admittance: if the couple took them in gladly, they all had a drink together. In that way they acquitted themselves of having taken a liberty without right, by disturbing the established pattern of normal mar-

Bastet, daughter of Râ, is often represented with a gold ring in one ear, gold being the symbol of the sun. XVIII Dynasty, Egypt.

The cat seated at
the foot of the
Tree of Knowledge.
Albrecht Dürer:
Adam and Eve.
Albertina, Vienna.

'Cat torments mouse as wife does husband' (French proverb).

'Cat torments mouse as wife does husband' (French proverb).

Second marriages gave rise to horse-play in which the cat played a prominent role. On the extreme right the man in the blue hat is wearing a cat mask. Bibliothèque Nationale, Paris.

Melancholy cats by
Watteau. Musée
Bonnat, Bayonne.

riage within an age-group. But if the couple became angry, the tumult continued for nine consecutive nights, and on the ninth evening the crowd hung a cat on a pole with plenty of matchwood and set it on fire. Burning the cat as the symbol of illicit love was another sign of disapproval. In so doing, no doubt the crowd thought they could burn the guardian spirit of the new home, to which this abnormal couple had no right.

Disapproval was likewise shown when widowers remarried, but the circumstances had to be exceptional, as, for example, an inordinate difference in age.

It is noticeable that in affairs of love, marriage, or remarriage, it was usually the woman who was in question. They compared her with the cat, which is why the cat takes part in the punishment of the adulteress. Both in ancient Egypt and the Islamic

109

Suzanne Valadon ▶
highlights the cat's
russet coat when
wishing to stress
the feeling of
luxury and comfort.

▲
The cat is at the
centre of Gauguin's
three questions:
'*D'où venons-nous…?*'
Tompkins
Collection, Arthur
Gordon Tompkins
Residuary Fund,
Museum of Fine
Arts, Boston.

▶
The cat associated
with repose and
voluptuousness.
Manet: *Olympia*.
Bibliothèque
Nationale, Paris.

La Ceinture de Chasteté: anonymous German seventeenth-century engraving. The cat mounts guard and adds his protection to the other precautions taken at the period.

world, the cat became the executioner of the unfaithful spouse. A woman accused of adultery was tied up in a sack with a cat and thrown into the sea. Only a few hundred years ago, the same custom was practised in southern Germany where the adulteress tied in the sack was torn to pieces by the terrified animal. It was still customary in Turkey less than a hundred years ago.

Although these barbaric customs have disappeared the cat is still undeniably linked in men's minds with loose women, as demonstrated by the following proverbs: 'He who has a cat for his friend will certainly marry an immoral woman'; 'A cat plays with a mouse, the woman with her husband'; and 'Women were made from the tail of the cat and are therefore more malicious than men.'

The cat is associated with love and adultery even in art. It appears in the borders of a sixteenth-century Flemish tapestry decorated with grotesques and entitled: *The Adulteress.* In the 18th century and in modern painting the cat is found in scenes of secret languor and quiet delight: paintings by Fragonard, Boucher, Watteau and, of the moderns, by Manet *(Olympia)*, Renoir *(Portrait of Julie Manet)* and Gauguin *(Le Repos).*

The customary punishment meted out to an adulteress in Turkey only one hundred years ago was to tie her up in a sack together with a live cat, and throw her into the sea. Drawing by Claude Estang after an engraving in the Bibliothèque Nationale, Paris.

VIII CONCLUSION

The differences in ideas and attitudes towards the cat throughout the ages have been so extreme as to lend support to Lorenz's view that the cat is not really a domestic animal, but a small wild animal accustomed to living with us—which would also explain its various functions in different civilizations. The cat has never been merely functional like the other domestic animals. Its wild nature has affinities with the neglected elements of our society—woman, the senses, and the life of the imagination. At the same time the characteristic, unchanging nature of the cat has become a secular symbol of the permanence of home. In our ever more mechanized lives, the cat is a constant reminder of the capricious, untamable side of nature.

Even in the most pampered homes, he never forgets his proud ancestor of the forest—the wild

Ulrich Boner: *Der Edelstein*, fifteenth-century illustrations taken from a copy of the fourteenth-century manuscript. Bürgerbibliothek, Berne. Mss. hist. helv. X.49.

113

cat. His carnivorous nature made him welcome and
even venerated at the hearth of Neolithic man
because he protected their corn against rodents. But
every peasant is a potential poacher and his traditional dislike of the wild cat lies only just below the
surface. Moreover the magnetism of the cat's personality soon had him associated with sorcerers, so
that for hundreds of years his life was threatened by
burning at the stake.

Throughout centuries and civilizations, the cat has
moved between heaven and hell, never knowing a
stable, continuous existence like the dog. Archaeological discoveries, it is true, clarify history and
explain the customs of their period, whereas nowadays that kind of information is transmitted by
artists and that is how we know that in the 19th century the cat reached a happier point in its career:
painters found a place for them in the most attractive

114

compositions of the day. They attempted to perpetuate the cats' lines and forms, considered it as of interest in its own right and for itself. We have only to look at studies by Géricault and Delacroix and later Steinlen, who spent much of his time drawing cats, to see this development.

The nineteenth- and then twentieth-century writers likewise create a more friendly world for the cat, its joys, suffering, comfort or wretchedness: 'The cat, aristocrat both in type and origin, which has been so greatly maligned, deserves our respect at least,' wrote Alexandre Dumas. And Balzac, in *Les Peines de Cœur d'une Chatte anglaise* touches on the realm of comparative psychology in describing how domestic animals come to adopt the character and behavior of their owners. To speak of modern literature and the cat inevitably evokes the memory of Colette,

One of the finest interpretations of the cat: *Le Chat Blanc* by Géricault.

The contented cat in Foujita's *Chat Endormi.*

'Making friends with a cat can only be a profitable experience' said Colette. *Chat* by Jacques Nam.

For Steinlen the cat was the subject of innumerable creations.

From the 19th
century on, the cat
never ceases to
appear in scenes of
everyday life.
Toulouse-Lautrec:
Le Motographe.

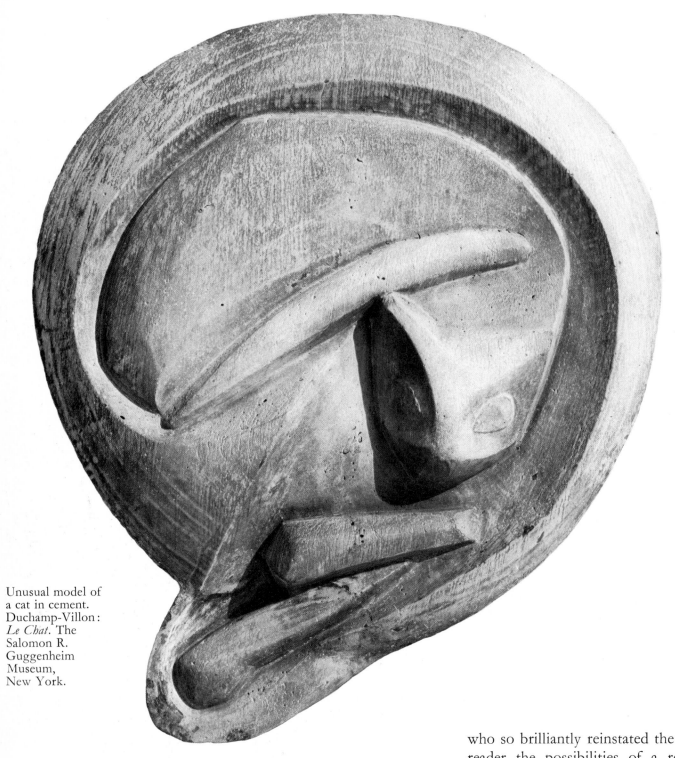

Unusual model of
a cat in cement.
Duchamp-Villon:
Le Chat. The
Salomon R.
Guggenheim
Museum,
New York.

who so brilliantly reinstated the cat by showing the
reader the possibilities of a relationship between
man and the animal. In *Les Vrilles de la Vigne* she
wrote: 'Making friends with a cat can only be a
profitable experience.' Consciously or unconsciously
she described in a single sentence the complex relations which have united man and the cat since their

The cat's enigmatic
nature both repels
and attracts—but
never leaves
indifferent.
Steinlen, 1896.

life together began—the enigmatic nature of the animal, attractive to some, repellent to others. Man always assumes that whatever attracts him must be beneficient, because emotional reasoning is as strong as logic today.

Rationalism tends to dominate the modern mind, whereas artists, who live in a world apart, will always think emotionally. Jean Cocteau wrote: 'I love cats because I love my home, and after a while they become its visible soul.' The visible soul of a house — and we have gone the full circle. We are back again to the cats' role as *Genius* of the home, a role he had held, as we have seen, at the dawn of time. He has found once again his rightful place and become what he was in Antiquity: the protective spirit of the home.

chat sauvag

Cats appreciate silence, as this one, turning its back on gossips. Hans Erni: *Caquetage de Femmes*.

The cat is not a domestic animal but a small, tame, wild beast. Drawings by Siné.

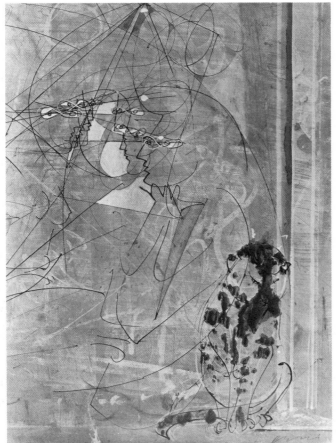

chat domestique

Man and cat. . .
together, for better
or worse. Fernand
Desnos: *La Chatte
blanche sous un
Parasol*. Petit Palais,
Geneva.

Imperturbable, the
cat continues on
its way.
Giacometti:
Le Chat.

ANTHOLOGY

Henri Rousseau:
Portrait de Pierre Loti.
Kunstmuseum,
Zurich.

CONTENTS OF THE ANTHOLOGY

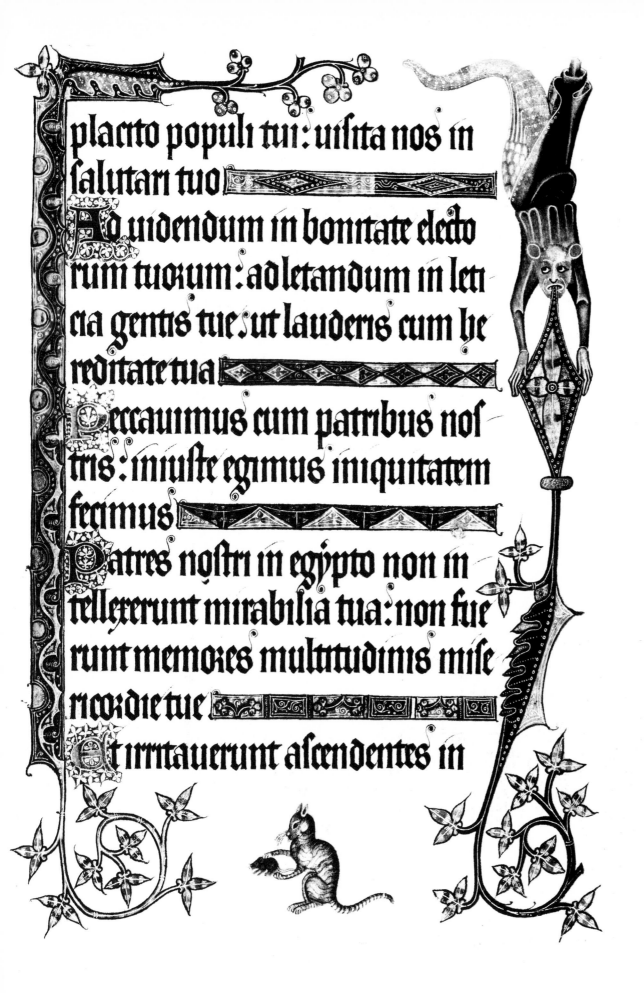

placito populi tui : uisita nos in
salutari tuo

Ad uidendum in bonitate electo
rum tuorum : ad letandum in leti
cia gentis tue : ut lauderis cum he
reditate tua

Peccauimus cum patribus nof
tris : iniuste egimus iniquitatem
fecimus

Patres nostri in egypto non in
tellexerunt mirabilia tua : non fue
runt memores multitudinis mise
ricordie tue

Et irritauerunt ascendentes in

LOVE AND LIFE

To the Right worshipfull Esquier
maister Iohn Yong, Grace and health.

I Have penned for your masterships pleasure one of
the stories which maister Streamer tolde the laste
Christmas, and which you so fain wold have heard
reported by master Feres him selfe. And although
I be unable to penne or speake it so pleasantly as he
could, yet have I so nerely used both the order and
wordes of him that spake them, which is not the
least vertue of a reporter that I doubt not that he and
master V Villot shal in the reading thinke they
haere master Streamer speake, and he him selfe in the
like action shal doubt whether he spaeketh or
readeth. I have devided his oration into three partes,
and put the argument before them, and an instruction
after them with such notes as might be gathered
thereof: so making it booke like, and intitled:
Beware the Cat. But because I doubt whether master
Streamer wilbe contented that other men plowe
with his oxen, I meane penne such. thinges as he
speaketh. . .

Beware the Cat,
1570.

A cat is a familiar and well knowne beast, called of the Haebrewes *Catull*, and *Schanar*, and *Schunara*; of the Graecians, Aeluros, and Kattes, and Katis, of the Saracens, *Katt*, the Italians *Gatta*, and *Gotto*. The Spaniards, *Gata* and *Gato*, the French, *Chat*; the Germanes, *Katz*; the Illyrians, *Kozka*; and *Furioz* (which is used for a cat by *Albertus Magnus*), and I conjecture to be either the Persian, or the Arabian worde. The Latines call it *Feles* and sometimes *Murilegus*, and *Musio*, because it catcheth Myce, but most commonly *Catus*, which is derived of *Cautus*, signifying wary: *Ovid* faith, that when the Gyantes warred with the Goddes, the Goddes put upon them the shapes of Beasts, and the sister of *Apollo* lay for a spy in the likenes of a cat, for a cat is a watchfull and warye beast, sildome overtaken, and most attendant to her sport and prey; according to that observation of *Mantuan*:

Non fecus ae miuricatus, ille, invadere pernam
Netitur, hic rimas occulis observat acutis.

And for this cause did the Egyptians place them for hallowed Beasts, and kept them in their Temples, although they alledged the use of their skinnes for the cover of shieldes which was but an unreasonable theft, for the softnesse of a cats skinne is not fit to defend or beare a blowe: It is knowne also that it was capitall among them, to kill an *Ibis*, and Aspe, a Crocodill, a Dogge or a Cat; insomuch as, that in the daies of the King *Ptolaemey*, when a peace was lately made between the Romaines and the Egyptians; and the Roman Ambassadors remaining still in Egypt, it is fortunes that a Romane unwares killed a cat, which being by the multitude of the Egyptians espied, they presently fell upon the Ambassadors house, to raze adown the same, except the offender might be delivered unto them, to suffer death: so that neither the honour of the Roman name, nor the

coulde haue reftrained them from that fury, had not rhe King himfelfe & his greateft Lords come in perfon, not fo much to deliuer the Roman Cat-murderer, as to fauegard him from the peoples violence; and not onely the [10] Egyptians were fooles in this kind, but the Arabians alfo, who worfhipped a cat for a God; and when the cat dyed, they mourned as much for her, as for the father of the family, fhauing the hair from their eye-lids, and carrying the beaft to the Tem- [20] ple, where the Priefts falted it and gaue it a holy funerall in *Bubaftum*: (which was a burying plaf for cattes neer the Altar) wherin may appeare to al men, in what miferable blindneffe the wifeft men of the world, (forfaking, or depriued of the true [30] knowledge of God are,) more then captiuated, fo that their wretched eftate cannot better bee expreffed then by the words of S. Paule, *When they thoght to be wife, they becam fools.*

The Histoire of Four-Footed Beastes, collected from the writings of Conrad Gesner and other authors, by Edward Topsall, Vol. I., 1658.

necessity of peace coulde have restrained them from that fury, had not the King himselfe & his greatest Lords come in person, not so much to deliver the Roman Car-murderer, as to safegard him from the peoples violence; and not only the Egyptians were fooles in this kinde but the Arabians also, who worshipped a Cat for a God; and when the Cat dyed, they mourned as much for her, as for the father of the family, shaving the hair from their eye-lids, carrying the beast to the Temple where the priests salted it and gave it a holy funerall in *Bubastum*: (which was a burying plac for cattes near the Altar) wherin may appear to al men, in what miserable blindnesse the wisest men of the world (forsaking or deprived of the true knowledge of God are,) more than captivated, so that their wretched estate cannot better bee expressed than by the wordes of S. Paule, *When they thougt to be wise, they becam fools*.

Once catters were all wilde, but afterward they retyred to houses, wherefore there are plenty of them in all countries: Martiall in an Epigram, celebrated a *Pannonian* cat with this diftichon:

Pannonicas nobis nunquam dedis umbria cattas
Manuls hac dominae mittere dona pudens.

The Spanish blacke cats are of most price among the Germaines, because they are nimblest and have the softest haire fit for garment.

A cat is in all partes like a Lyonesse (except in her sharpe eares) wherefore the Poets faine, that when *Venus* had turned a cat into a beautifull woman (calling her *Aelures*) who forgetting her good turne, contended with the goddesse for beauty: in indignation whereof, she returned her to her first nature, only making her outward shape to resemble a lyon, which is not altogither idle, but may admonish the wisest, that faire and foule, men and beasts, hold nothing by their owne worth and benefit, but by vertue of their creator: Wherefore if at any time they rise against their maker, let them looke to loose their honour and dignity in their beste part and to returne to basenes and inglorious contempt out of which they were first taken, and howsoever their outwarde shape and condition please them, yet at the best they are but beastes that perish, for the Lyons suffer hunger.

128

THE CATS CONCERT

Gremalkin one day as reclin'd by the Fire.
Conversing with one of her Kittens close by her.
Resolv'd like her Neighbors her taste to Display.
And to reval their Fetes and their Frolics so gay.

With Musics rich charms and with rapture exclaim'd.
To her daughter in Fashions bright annals long
                                            [famed.
My Friend I'll invite and a Concert well make.
On purpose to shew off your wonderfull shake.

A Voice such as Yours must astonish the Town.
When they hear your deep base and your fine Treble
                                            [Tone.
Tones surely bestow'd like the Syrens of Yore.
To prove ever Mortals their Majical power.

Your brother black Tommy shall play on the Flute.
And woe be to him who makes any dispute.
Your Father if cured of the pain in his Face
Which visit Gremalkin as well as his Grace
Shall give us a Tune on his new Double Bass.

Whilst our sweet tabby Neighbours shall lend us
                                            [assistance.
That the charm of our Consert may pass all resistance
A Supper was orderd most costly and rare.
Tho tis hinted they borrow'd the smart bill of Fare.

Of some friends of high taste and still higher
                                            [connections.
But the Muse scorns to mention such cruel
                                            [reflections.
Toasted Cheese, in the middle a favorite Dish.
Was supported on Each side by Liver and Fish.

FRONTISPIECE.

"The Cats' Concert", *The Butterfly's Ball and Other Tales,* 1807/08.

At the Top with the happiest arranged was placed.
Concealing their Charms in a cover of Paste.
A small dish of Sparrow just strayd from their Nest.
With harricoed Mice so dilisiously Dress'd.

That report which talked much of the exquisite fare.
Declared many An Alderman sigh'd to be there.
The Kitten in hast all her powers to display.
In a Moment to practice her part frisk'd away.
But little Black Tommy was ordered to stay.

THE WHITE CAT

When his dress was complete, they conducted him to an apartment he had not yet seen, and which also was magnificiently furnished. There was in it a table spread for a repast, and every thing upon it was of the purest gold, adorned with jewels. The Prince observed there were two covers set; and was wondering who was to be his companion, when a great number of cats marched by two and two into the room, and placed themselves in an orchestra at one end of it; some had books, which contained the strangest-looking notes he had ever seen; others guitars; and one of them held a roll of paper with which he began to beat the time, while the rest played a concert of music.

As he was reflecting on the wonderful things he had seen in this palace, his attention was suddenly caught by a small figure, which just then entered the room, and advanced towards him. It wore a long black veil, and was supported by two cats in mourning, and with swords by their sides; they were followed by a numerous retinue of cats, some carrying cages full of rats, and others mouse-traps full of mice.

The Prince was at a loss what to think. The little figure now approached, and throwing aside her veil, he beheld a most beautiful white cat: she seemed young and melancholy, and addressing herself to the Prince, she said, 'Young Prince, you are welcome; your presence affords me the greatest pleasure.'— 'Madam,' replied the Prince, 'I would fain thank you for your generosity, nor can I help observing that you must be a most extraordinary creature, to possess, with your present form, the gift of speech. . .'

THE EAGLE, THE CAT, AND THE SOW

An Eagle had built her nest upon the top branches of an old oak; a wild Cat inhabited a hole in the middle; and in the hollow part at the bottom, was a Sow, with a whole litter of pigs. A happy neighbourhood; and might long have continued so, had it not been for the wicked insinuations of the designing Cat. For, first of all, up she crept to the Eagle; and, 'good neighbour,' says she, 'we shall be all undone: that filthy Sow yonder, does nothing but lie routing at the foot of the tree, and, as I suspect, intends to grub it up, that she may the more easily come at our young ones. For my part, I will take care of my own concerns; you may do as you please, but I will watch her motions, though I stay at home this month for it.' When she had said this, which could not fail of putting the Eagle into a great fright, down she went, and made a visit to the Sow at the bottom; and, putting on a sorrowful face, 'I hope,' says she, 'you do not intend to go abroad to-day?' 'Why not?' says the Sow. 'Nay,' replies the other, 'you may do as you please; but I overheard the Eagle tell her young ones, that she would treat them with a pig, the first time she saw you go out; and I am not sure but she may take up with a kitten in the mean time; so, good-morrow to you; you will excuse me, I must go and take care of the little folks at home.' Away she went accordingly; and, by contriving to steal out softly at nights for her prey, and to stand watching and peeping all day at her hole, as under great concern, she made such an impression upon the Eagle and the Sow, that neither of them dared to venture abroad, for fear of the other. The consequence of which was, that themselves and their young ones, in a little time were all starved, and made prizes of, by the treacherous Cat and her kittens.

REFLECTION

There can be no peace in any state or family where whisperers and tale-bearers are encouraged.

"The Eagle, the Cat and the Sow", *Select Fables,* by Thomas and John Bewick, 1820.

THE TRAVELLING MUSICIANS, OR THE WAITS OF BREMEN

An honest farmer had once an ass, that had been a faithful servant to him a great many years, but was now growing old and every day more and more unfit for work. His master therefore was tired of keeping him and began to think of putting an end to him; but the ass, who saw that some mischief was in the wind, took himself slyly off, and began his journey towards Bremen, 'for there,' thought he, 'I may chance to be chosen town-musician.'

After he had travelled a little way, he spied a dog lying by the road-side and painting as if he were very tired. 'What makes you pant so, my friend?' said the ass. 'Alas!' said the dog, 'my master was going to knock me on the head, because I am old and weak, and can no longer make myself useful to him in hunting; so I ran away: but what can I do to earn my livelihood?' 'Hark ye!' said the ass, 'I am going to Bremen to turn musician: suppose you go with me, and try what you can do in the same way?' The dog said he was willing, and they jogged on together.

They had not gone far before they saw a cat sitting in the middle of the road and making a most rueful face. 'Pray, my good lady,' said the ass, 'what's the matter with you? you look quite out of spirits!' 'Ah me!' said the cat, 'how can one be in good spirits when one's life is in danger? Because I am beginning to grow old, and had rather lie at my ease by the fire than run about the house after the mice, my mistress laid hold of me, and was going to drown me; and though I have been lucky enough to get away from her, I do not know what I am to live upon.' 'Oh!' said the ass, 'by all means go with us to Bremen; you are a good night singer, and may make your fortune as one of the waits.' The cat was pleased with the thought, and joined the party.

Soon afterwards, as they were passing by a farm-yard, they saw a cock perched upon a gate, and screaming out with all his might and main. 'Bravo!' said the ass; 'upon my word you make a famous noise; pray what is all this about?' 'Why,' said the cock, 'I was just now saying that we should have fine weather for our washing-day, and yet my mistress and the cook don't thank me for my pains, but threaten to cut off my head tomorrow, and make broth of me for the guests that are coming on Sunday!' 'Heaven forbid!' said the ass; 'come with us, Master Chanticleer: it will be better, at any rate, than staying here to have your head cut off! Besides, who knows? If we take care to sing in tune, we may get up a concert of our own: so come along with us.' 'With all my heart,' said the cock: so they all four went on jollily together.

They could not, however, reach the town the first day; so when night came on, they went into a wood to sleep. The ass and the dog laid themselves down under a great tree, and the cat climbed up into the branches; while the cock, thinking that the higher he sat the safer he should be, flew up to the very top of the tree, and then, according to his custom, before he went to sleep, looked out on all sides of him to see that every thing was well. In doing this, he saw afar off something bright and shining; and calling to his companions said, 'There must be a house no great way off, for I see a light.' 'If that be the case,' said the ass, 'we had better change our quarters, for our lodging is not the best in the world!' 'Besides,' added the dog, 'I should not be the worse for a bone or two, or a bit of meat.' So they walked off together towards the spot where Chanticleer had seen the light; and as they drew near, it became larger and brighter, till they at last came close to a house in which a gang of robbers lived.

The ass, being the tallest of the company, marched up to the window and peeped in. 'Well, Donkey,' said Chanticleer, 'what do you see?' 'What do I see?' replied the ass, 'why I see a table spread with all kinds of good things, and robbers sitting round it making merry.' 'That would be a noble lodging for us,' said the cock. 'Yes,' said the ass, 'if we could only get in': so they consulted together how they should contrive to get the robbers out; and at last they hit upon a plan. The ass placed himself upright on his hind-legs, with his fore-feet resting against the window; the dog got upon his back; the cat scrambled up to the dog's shoulders, and the cock flew up and sat upon the cat's head. When all was ready, a signal was given, and they began their music. The ass brayed, the dog barked, the cat mewed, and the cock screamed; and then they all broke through the window at once, and came tumbling into the room, amongst the broken glass, with a most hideous clatter! The robbers, who had been not a little frightened by the opening concert, had now no doubt that some frightful hobgoblin had broken in upon them, and scampered away as fast as they could.

The coast once clear, our travellers soon sat down, and dispatched what the robbers had left, with as much eagerness as if they had not expected to eat again for a month. As soon as they had satisfied themselves, they put out the lights, and each once more sought out a resting-place to his own liking. The donkey laid himself down upon a heap of straw in the yard; the dog stretched himself upon a mat behind the door; the cat rolled herself up on the hearth before the warm ashes; and the cock perched upon a beam on the top of the house; and, as they were all rather tired with their journey, they soon fell asleep.

But about midnight, when the robbers saw from afar that the lights were out and that all seemed quiet, they began to think that they had been in too great a hurry to run away; and one of them, who was bolder than the rest, went to see what was going on. Finding every thing still, he marched into the kitchen, and groped about till he found a match in order to light a candle; and then, espying the glittering fiery eyes of the cat, he mistook them for live coals, and held the match to them to light it. But the cat, not understanding this joke, sprung at his face, and spit, and scratched at him. This frightened him dreadfully, and away he ran to the back door; but there the dog jumped up and bit him in the leg; and as he was crossing over the yard the ass kicked him; and the cock, who had been awakened by the noise, crowed with all his might. At this the robber ran back as fast as he could to his comrades, and told the captain 'how a horrid witch had got into the house, and had spit at him and scratched his face with her long bony fingers; how a man with a knife in his hand had hidden himself behind the door, and stabbed him in the leg; how a black monster stood in the yard and struck him with a club; and how the devil sat upon the top of the house and cried out, "Throw the rascal up here!"' After this the robbers never dared to go back to the house: but the musicians were so pleased with their quarters, that they took up their abode there; and there they are, I dare say, at this very day.

THE CAT'S PILGRIMAGE

... The Cat made two great arches with her back and her tail.

'Bless the mother that laid you,' said she. 'You were dropped by mistake in a goose nest. You won't do. I don't know much, but I am not such a creature as you, anyhow. A great white thing!'

She straightened her body, stuck her tail up on end, and marched off with much dignity. But, though she respected herself rather more than before, she was not on the way to the end of her difficulties. She tried all the creatures she met without advancing a step. They had all the old story, 'Do your duty.' But each had its own, and no one could tell her what hers was. Only one point they all agreed upon—the duty of getting their dinner when they were hungry. The day wore on, and she began to think she would like hers. Her meals came so regularly at home that she scarcely knew what hunger was; but now the sensation came over her very palpably, and she experienced quite new emotions as the hares and rabbits skipped about her, or as she spied a bird upon a tree. For a moment she thought she would go back and eat the Owl—he was the most useless creature she had seen; but on second thoughts she didn't fancy he would be nice: besides that, his claws were sharp and his beak too. Presently, however, as she sauntered down the path, she came on a little open patch of green, in the middle of which a fine fat Rabbit was sitting. There was no escape. The path ended there, and the bushes were so thick on each side that he couldn't get away except through her paws.

'Really,' said the Cat, 'I don't wish to be troublesome; I wouldn't do it if I could help it; but I am very hungry, I am afraid I must eat you. It is very unpleasant, I assure you, to me as well as to you.'

The poor Rabbit begged for mercy.

'Well,' said she, 'I think it is hard; I do really—and, if the law could be altered, I should be the first to welcome it. But what can a Cat do? You eat the grass; I eat you. But, Rabbit, I wish you would do me a favour.'

'Anything to save my life,' said the Rabbit.

'It is not exactly that,' said the Cat; 'but I haven't been used to killing my own food, and it is disagreeable. Couldn't you die? I shall hurt you dreadfully if I kill you.'

'Oh!' said the Rabbit, 'you are a kind Cat; I see it in your eyes, and your whiskers don't curl like those of the cats in the woods. I am sure you will spare me.'

'But, Rabbit, it is a question of principle. I have to

The Cat's Pilgrimage,
by James Anthony
Froude, illustrations
by J.B., 1870.

"I have seven little ones at home and they will all die without me. *Pray let me go*."

do my duty; and the only duty I have, as far as I can make out, is to get my dinner.'

'If you kill me, Cat, to do your duty, I sha'n't be able to do mine.'

It was a doubtful point, and the Cat was new to casuistry. 'What is your duty?' said she.

'I have seven little ones at home—seven little ones, and they will all die without me. Pray let me go.'

'What! do you take care of your children?' said the Cat. 'How interesting! I should like to see that; take me.'

'Oh! you would eat them, you would,' said the Rabbit. 'No! better eat me than them. No, no.'

'Well, well,' said the Cat, 'I don't know; I suppose I couldn't answer for myself. I don't think I am right, for duty is pleasant, and it is very unpleasant to be so hungry; but I suppose you must go. You seem a good Rabbit. Are you happy, Rabbit?'

'Happy! oh, dear beautiful Cat! if you spare me to my poor babies!'

'Pooh, pooh!' said the Cat, peevishly; 'I don't want fine speeches; I meant whether you thought it worth while to be alive! Of course you do! It don't matter. Go, and keep out of my way; for, if I doesn't find something to eat, you may not get off another time. Get along, Rabbit!'

WHITTINGTON AND HIS CAT

Little Dick would have lived very happy in this good family if it had not been for the ill-natured cook, who was finding fault and scolding him from morning to night, and besides, she was so fond of basting, that when she had no meat to baste, she would baste poor Dick's head and shoulders with a broom, or anything else that happened to fall in her way. At last her ill-usage of him was told to Alice, Mr. Fitzwarren's daughter, who told the cook she should be turned away if she did not treat him kinder.

The ill-humour of the cook was now a little amended; but besides this Dick had another hardship to get over. His bed stood in a garret, where there were so many holes in the floor and the walls that every night he was tormented with rats and mice. A gentleman having given Dick a penny for cleaning his shoes, he thought he would buy a cat with it. The next day he saw a girl with a cat, and asked her if she would let him have it for a penny. The girl said she would, and at the same time told him the cat was an excellent mouser.

Dick hid his cat in the garret, and always took care to carry a part of his dinner to her; and in a short time he had no more trouble with the rats and mice, but slept quite sound every night.

Soon after this, his master had a ship ready to sail; and as he thought it right that all his servants should have some change for good fortune as well as himself, he called them all into the parlour and asked them what they would send out.

They all had something that they were willing to venture except poor Dick, who had neither money nor goods, and therefore could send nothing.

For this reason he did not come into the parlour with the rest; but Miss Alice guessed what was the matter, and ordered him to be called in. She then said she would lay down some money for him, from her own purse; but the father told her this would not do, for it must be something of his own.

When poor Dick heard this, he said he had nothing but a cat which he bought for a penny some time since of a little girl.

'Fetch your cat then, my good boy,' said Mr. Fitzwarren, 'and let her go.'

Dick went upstairs and brought down poor puss, with tears in his eyes, and gave her to the captain; for he said he should now be kept awake again all night by the rats and mice.

All the company laughed at Dick's odd venture; and Miss Alice, who felt pity for the poor boy, gave him some money to buy another cat.

This, and many other marks of kindness shown him by Miss Alice, made the ill-tempered cook jealous of poor Dick, and she began to use him more cruelly than ever, and always made game of him for sending his cat to sea. She asked him if he thought his cat would sell for as much money as would buy a stick to beat him.

At last poor Dick could not bear this usage any longer, and he thought he would run away from his place; so he packed up his few things, and started very early in the morning, on All-hallows Day, which is the first of November. He walked as far as Hollo-way; and there sat down on a stone, which to this day is called Whittington's stone, and began to think to himself which road he should take as he proceeded onwards.

While he was thinking what he should do, the Bells of Bow Church, which at that time had only six, began to ring, and he fancied their sound seemed to say to him:

Turn again, Whittington,
Lord Mayor of London.

'Lord Mayor of London!' said he to himself. 'Why, to be sure, I would put up with almost anything now, to be Lord Mayor of London, and ride in a fine coach, when I grow to be a man! Well, I will go back, and think nothing of the cuffing and scolding of the old cook, if I am to be Lord Mayor of London at last.'

Dick went back, and was lucky enough to get into the house, and set about his work, before the old cook came downstairs.

The ship, with the cat on board, was a long time at sea; and was at last driven by the winds on a part of the coast of Barbary, where the only people were the Moors, that the English had never known before.

The people then came in great numbers to see the sailors, who were of different colour to themselves, and treated them very civilly; and, when they became better acquainted, were very eager to buy the fine things that the ship was loaded with.

When the captain saw this, he sent patterns of the best things he had to the king of the country; who was so much pleased with them, that he sent for the captain to the palace. Here they were placed, as it is the custom of the country, on rich carpets marked with gold and silver flowers. The king and queen were seated at the upper end of the room; and a number of dishes were brought in for dinner. They had not sat long, when a vast number of rats and mice rushed in, helping themselves from almost every dish. The captain wondered at this, and asked if these vermin were not very unpleasant.

'Oh yes,' said they, 'very offensive; and the king would give half his treasure to be freed of them, for they not only destroy his dinner, as you see, but they assault him in his chamber, and even in bed, so that he is obliged to be watched while he is sleeping for fear of them.'

The captain jumped for joy; he remembered poor Whittington and his cat, and told the king he had a creature on board the ship that would despatch all these vermin immediately. The king's heart heaved so high at the joy which this news gave him that his turban dropped off his head. 'Bring this creature to me,' says he; 'vermin are dreadful in a court, and if she will perform what you say, I will load your ship with gold and jewels in exchange for her.'

The captain, who knew his business, took this opportunity to set forth the merits of Miss Puss. He told his majesty that it would be inconvenient to part with her, as, when she was gone, the rats and mice might destroy the goods in the ship—but to oblige his majesty he would fetch her. 'Run, run!' said the queen; 'I am impatient to see the dear creature.'

Away went the captain to the ship, while another dinner was got ready. He put puss under his arm, and arrived at the place soon enough to see the table full of rats.

When the cat saw them, she did not wait for bidding, but jumped out of the captain's arms, and in a few minutes laid almost all the rats and mice dead at her feet. The rest of them in their fright scampered away to their holes.

The king and queen were quite charmed to get so easily rid of such plagues, and desired that the creature who had done them so great a kindness might be brought to them for inspection. Upon which the captain called: 'Pussy, pussy, pussy!' and she came to him. He then presented her to the queen, who started back, and was afraid to touch a creature who had made such a havoc among the rats and mice. However, when the captain stroked the cat and called: 'Pussy, pussy,' the queen also touched her and cried: 'Putty, putty,' for she had not learned English. He then put her down on the queen's lap, where she, purring, played with her majesty's hand, and then sung herself to sleep.

The king, having seen the exploits of Mrs. Puss, and being informed that she was with young, and would stock the whole country, bargained with the captain for the whole ship's cargo, and then gave him ten times as much for the cat as all the rest amounted to.

"Whittington and his Cat", *English Folk and Fairy Tales*, by E.S. Hartland. Illustrations by G.E. Brock, 1890.

The captain then took leave of the royal party, and set sail with a fair wind for England, and after a happy voyage arrived safe in London.

One morning Mr. Fitzwarren had just come to his counting-house and seated himself at the desk, when somebody came tap, tap, at the door. 'Who's there?' says Mr. Fitzwarren. 'A friend,' answered the other; 'I come to bring you good news of your ship *Unicorn.*' The merchant, bustling up instantly, opened the door, and who should be seen waiting but the captain and factor, with a cabinet of jewels, and a bill of lading, for which the merchant lifted up his eyes and thanked heaven for sending him such a prosperous voyage.

They then told the story of the cat, and showed the rich present that the king and queen had sent for her to poor Dick. As soon as the merchant heard this, he called out to his servants:

Go fetch him—we will tell him of the same;
Pray call him Mr. Whittington by name.

Mr. Fitzwarren now showed himself to be a good man; for when some of his servants said so great a treasure was too much for him, he answered: 'God forbid I should deprive him of the value of a single penny.'

He then sent for Dick, who at that time was scouring pots for the cook, and was quite dirty.

Mr. Fitzwarren ordered a chair to be set for him, and so he began to think they were making game of him, at the same time begging them not to play tricks with a poor simple boy, but to let him go down again, if they pleased, to his work.

'Indeed, Mr. Whittington,' said the merchant, 'we are all quite in earnest with you, and I most heartily rejoice in the news these gentlemen have brought you; for the captain has sold your cat to the King of Barbary, and brought you in return for her more riches than I possess in the whole world; and I wish, you may long enjoy them!'

Sur les Chats de l'autre page.

Je les aime et je les déteste ces animaux charmants et perfides. J'ai plaisir à les toucher, à faire glisser sous ma main leur poil soyeux qui craque, à sentir leur chaleur dans ce poil, dans cette fourrure fine, exquise ; car rien n'est plus doux, rien ne donne à la peau une sensation plus délicate, plus raffinée plus rare que la robe tiède et vibrante d'un chat. Mais elle me met aux doigts, cette robe vivante, un désir étrange et féroce d'étrangler la bête que je caresse. Je sens en elle l'envie qu'elle a de me mordre et de me déchirer ; je la sens et je la prends, cette envie, comme un fluide qu'elle me communique ; je la prends par le bout de mes doigts dans ce poil chaud ; et elle monte ; elle monte le long de mes nerfs, le long de mes membres, jusqu'à mon cœur, jusqu'à ma tête ; elle m'emplit, court le long de ma peau, fait se serrer mes dents. Et toujours, toujours, au bout de mes dix doigts je sens le chatouillement vif et léger qui me pénètre et m'envahit.

27 Avril 1896

Guy de Maupassant

Page from the Visitor's Book of Waddesdon Manor, Aylesbury (England). Text by Guy de Maupassant on an illustration by Guy Lambert, 1886.

THE OWL AND THE PUSSY-CAT

I.

The Owl and the Pussy-Cat went to sea
   In a beautiful pea-green boat,
   They took some honey, and plenty of
     money,
Wrapped up in a five-pound note.
The Owl looked up to the stars above,
   And sang to a small guitar,
'O lovely Pussy! O Pussy, my love,
   'What a beautiful Pussy you are,
     'You are,
     'You are!
'What a beautiful Pussy you are!'

III.

'Dear Pig, are you willing to sell for one shilling
   Your ring?' Said the Piggy, 'I will.'
So they took it away, and were married next day
   By the Turkey who lives on the hill.
They dined on mince, and slices of quince,
   Which they ate with a runcible spoon;
And hand in hand, on the edge of the sand,
   They danced by the light of the moon,
     The moon,
     The moon,
They danced by the light of the moon.

II.

Pussy said to the Owl, 'You elegant fowl!
   'How charmingly sweet you sing!
'O let us be married! too long we have tarried
   'But what shall we do for a ring?'
They sailed away for a year and a day,
   To the land where the Bong-tree grows,
And there in a wood a Piggy-wig stood,
   With a ring at the end of his nose,
     His nose,
     His nose,
With a ring at the end of his nose.

"The Owl and the Pussy Cat", *Nonsense Omnibus,* by Edward Lear, illustrations by Lear.

PUSS IN BOOTS

And so Puss set out on his expedition.

Now he had put some bran and parsley into his bag, and, trotting on till he came to a rabbit-warren, he put it down open (retaining, however, the strings of it), and hid himself amongst the ferns and the bushes.

By-and-by, two fat giddy young rabbits crept into the bag.

Puss instantly drew the strings tightly, and then hurried off till he reached the king's palace. Arriving at the gate he demanded an audience of the sovereign.

The attendants were so amazed at hearing a cat talk, that they reported the demand to the king, and the royal curiosity was aroused so greatly by the story of a talking cat, that he at once desired them to admit Pussy.

Pussy walked through the palace with graceful nonchalance, stroking his moustache, and casting civil glances of contempt on everything round him, till he stood in the royal presence. Then he bowed very low; and on the king's asking from whence he came, and what was his business, he replied:

'Please your majesty, my master, the Marquis of Carabas' (this was the title he chose to confer on Gabriel), 'sends me with these rabbits as a present to your majesty, with the assurance of his entire devotion.'

'Tell my lord marquis,' replied the astonished king, 'that I am much obliged for his gift; and especially pleased that he should have sent it by such a courteous messenger. Pray may I ask what country produced so accomplished a feline courtier?'

'Your majesty is too good! I am a native of Katland; only a poor cat, in fact. But my master is exceedingly *recherché* in his tastes; and as he thinks footmen are grown vulgar, he has engaged my services instead.'

'Indeed! has he a household composed of talking cats, then?'

'No, my liege; his servants are invisible, except myself. He thinks it more elegant to have repose and little show in his dwelling than visible attendants.'

'A man of first-rate taste!' exclaimed the king. 'Why does he not come to court?'

Puss stroked his moustache.

'Really—ahem! Your majesty is doomed by your royal state to endure it; and moreover, you are too great to be affected by such contact—but there is such a mixture at courts!'

Now the king of that country, happening to be rather silly, thought that the Marquis of Carabas

"Puss in Boots", *Fairy Library*, illustrations by H.M. Brock, 1907.

143

must needs be a very grand person; so he dismissed Puss with many compliments, and a purse of gold. The cat went directly to a cook's shop, bought a fricasse for his master's dinner, and some cat's-meat for himself, and went home quite joyful.

The next day he went into the ogre's preserves, which were wonderfully well kept, as no one ever dared go into them; and baiting his bag with wheat this time, he contrived to catch two partridges.

With these he again proceeded to the palace, was once more admitted, and gave the same message.

The king detained him to have a chat; for, as his majesty justly observed, you may talk to a man any day, but a cat is a different thing.

THE CAT THAT WALKED BY HIMSELF

This is the picture of the Cat that Walked by Himself, walking by his wild lone through the Wet Wild Woods and waving his wild tail. There is nothing else in the picture except some toadstools. They had to grow there because the woods were so wet. The lumpy thing on the low branch isn't a bird. It is moss that grew there because the Wild Woods were so wet.

Underneath the truly picture is a picture of the cosy Cave that the Man and the Woman went to after the Baby came. It was their summer Cave, and they planted wheat in front of it. The Man is riding on the Horse to find the Cow and bring her back to the Cave to be milked. He is holding up his hand to call the Dog, who has swum across to the other side of the river, looking for rabbits.

BUSTOPHER JONES: THE CAT ABOUT TOWN

Bustopher Jones is *not* skin and bones—
In fact, he's remarkably fat.
He doesn't haunt pubs—he has eight or nine clubs,
For he's the St. James's Street Cat!
He's the Cat we all greet as he walks down the street
In his coat of fastidious black:
No commonplace mousers have such well-cut
                                 [trousers
Or such an impeccable back.
In the whole of St. James's the smartest of names is
The name of this Brummell of Cats;
And we're all of us proud to be nodded or bowed to
By Bustopher Jones in white spats!

His visits are occasional to the *Senior Educational*
And it is against the rules
For any one Cat to belong both to that
And the *Joint Superior Schools.*
For a similar reason, when game is in season
He is found, not at *Fox's*, but *Blimp's*;
He is frequently seen at the gay *Stage and Screen*
Which is famous for winkles and shrimps.
In the season of venison he gives his ben'son
To the *Pothunter's* succulent bones;
And just before noon's not a moment to soon
To drop in for a drink at the *Drones.*

When he's seen in a hurry there's probably curry
At the *Siamese*—or at the *Glutton*;
If he looks full of gloom then he's lunched at the
                                 [*Tomb*
On cabbage, rice pudding and mutton.

So, much in this way, passes Bustopher's day—
At one club or another he's found.
It can be no surprise that under our eyes
He has grown unmistakably round.

at that
by Himself",
Stories by
d Kipling,

He's a twenty-five pounder, or I am a bounder,
And he's putting on weight every day:
But he's so well preserved because he's observed
All his life a routine, so he'll say.
Or, to put it in rhyme: 'I shall last out my time'
Is the word of this stoutest of Cats.
It must and it shall be Spring in Pall Mall
While Bustopher Jones wears white spats!

"Bustopher Jones: The Cat About Town", *Old Possums Book of Practical Cats*, by T.S. Eliot, illustrations by Osbert Lancaster. With kind permission of Faber and Faber.

PIG AND PEPPER

'——so long as I get *somewhere*,' Alice added as an explanation.

'Oh, you're sure to do that,' said the Cat, 'if you only walk long enough.'

Alice felt that this could not be denied, so she tried another question. 'What sort of people live about here?'

'In *that* direction,' the Cat said, waving its right paw round, 'lives a Hatter: and in *that* direction,' waving the other paw, 'lives a March Hare. Visit either you like: they're both mad.'

'But I don't want to go among mad people,' Alice remarked.

'Oh, you ca'n't help that,' said the Cat: 'we're all mad here. I'm mad. You're mad.'

'How do you know I'm mad?' said Alice.

'You must be,' said the Cat, 'or you wouldn't have come here.'

Alice didn't think that proved it at all: however, she went on: 'And how do you know that you're mad?'

'To begin with,' said the Cat, 'a dog's not mad. You grant that?'

'I suppose so,' said Alice.

'Well, then,' the Cat went on, 'you see a dog growls when it's angry, and wags its tail when it's pleased. Now *I* growl when I'm pleased, and wag my tail when I'm angry. Therefore I'm mad.'

'*I* call it purring, not growling,' said Alice.

'Call it what you like,' said the Cat. 'Do you play croquet with the Queen to-day?'

'I should like it very much,' said Alice, 'but I haven't been invited yet.'

'You'll see me there,' said the Cat, and vanished.

Alice was not much surprised at this, she was getting so well used to queer things happening. While she was still looking at the place where it had been, it suddenly appeared again.

'By-the-bye, what became of the baby?' said the Cat. 'I'd nearly forgotten to ask.'

'It turned into a pig.' Alice answered very quietly, just as if the Cat had come back in a natural way.

'I thought it would,' said the Cat, and vanished again.

146

" But I don't want to go among mad people," Alice remarked.

" Oh, you ca'n't help that," said the Cat : " we're all mad here. I'm mad. You're mad."

" How do you know I'm mad ? " said Alice.

" You must be," said the Cat, " or you wouldn't have come here."

Alice didn't think that proved it at all : how-

rug, all knots and tangles, with the kitten running after its own tail in the middle.

'Oh, you wicked wicked little thing!' cried Alice, catching up the kitten, and giving it a little kiss to make it understand that it was in disgrace. 'Really, Dinah ought to have taught you better manners! You *ought*, Dinah, you know you ought!' she added, looking reproachfully at the old cat, and speaking in as cross a voice as she could manage—and then she scrambled back into the arm-chair, taking the kitten and the worsted with her, and began winding up the ball again. But she didn't get on very fast, as she was talking all the time, sometimes to the kitten, and sometimes to herself. Kitty sat very demurely on her knee, pretending to watch the progress of the winding, and now and then putting out one paw and gently touching the ball, as if it would be glad to help if it might.

LOOKING-GLASS HOUSE

One thing was certain, that the *white* kitten had had nothing to do with it: — it was the black kitten's fault entirely. For the white kitten had been having its face washed by the old cat for the last quarter of an hour (and bearing it pretty well, considering); so you see that it *couldn't* have had any hand in the mischief.

The way Dinah washed her children's faces was this: first she held the poor thing down by its ear with one paw, and then with the other paw she rubbed its face all over, the wrong way, beginning at the nose: and just now, as I said, she was hard at work on the white kitten, which was lying quite still and trying to purr—no doubt feeling that it was all meant for its good.

But the black kitten had been finished with earlier in the afternoon, and so, while Alice was sitting curled up in a corner of the great arm-chair, half talking to herself and half asleep, the kitten had been having a grand game of romps with the ball of worsted Alice had been trying to wind up, and had been rolling it up and down till it had all come undone again; and there it was, spread over the hearth-

"Looking Glass House", *Alice through the Looking Glass,* by Lewis Carroll, illustrations by John Tenniel.

THE CAT
IN THE HOME

THE PSYCHOLOGY OF THE CAT

Much has been written about the life and habits of the cat, but it is difficult to establish any rules or precise limits, because generalizations can rarely be applied to cats. Every cat is different and all behave differently. The only thing they have in common is that they are solitary animals that can sometimes be brought to live together.

The psychology of these self-sufficient creatures is extremely complex; it is more complicated than that of the dog, with which it is often compared, and has therefore been somewhat neglected. To embark on a discussion of cat psychology in any depth would be beyond the confines of this work, so that I propose to do no more than touch on the main aspects of the animal's nature.

LANGUAGE

'Cats undoubtedly talk and reason among themselves,' wrote Montaigne, and it is true that the cat knows how to express its wishes by its voice. The cat miaows, and with a great variety of expressions, however monotonous they may seem. There is, for instance, the call of the male to the female, or the different ways the mother talks to her kittens, and the whole range of voice tones the animal uses if he is hungry, thirsty, or wants to come in or out or communicate any other whim. There are cries of happiness and pain, bad-tempered growls, and hissing and spitting from fear or anger. There is the purr of contentment, and the very special sound the cat reserves for greeting his owner.

Observers have recorded that the cat's vocabulary contains sixty-three sounds. There is no doubt that he has a language for communicating with man and with other cats.

Cats are 'lone
wolves.'

PLAY

For every living creature, man or animal, play is an apprenticeship for life. It helps to develop both physique and instinct—which explains why a kitten chases a leaf, a cork or a ball, just as it will later pounce on a mouse. Schiller and Herbert Spencer both considered play was a release of pent-up energy. For man and all the higher animals, the activity involved in playing uses up the stores of energy which have not been exhausted in the ordinary course of the day. The two theories are not incompatible but complementary: as the cat develops its faculties, it keeps fit by burning up excess energy.

As a predator, the cat reacts only to moving objects. It is life, or the semblance of life that captures his attention, excites his curiosity and stirs him into activity. Immobile objects leave him cold.

When kittens play together or when a kitten plays with his mother, they are preparing for the future battles of adult life by learning all the movements necessary for attack and defense. When two cats play together, they are well aware that their game is not in earnest. They may seem rough but neither gets hurt. Like Judo players, the dominant cat lets go when the other growls in a special way to show that it has had enough. The cat is a gentleman, proved by his sense of fairplay.

CHARACTER

Critics of the cat tend to boast of the qualities they admire in the dog. The parallel arises because the dog and the cat are the only animals that live freely by man's side, sharing his life and serving him willingly. However, that is their only point of similarity since their characters are otherwise quite different. The dog is truly domesticated, while the cat—and this should never be forgotten—is a wild animal who retains its proud, independent, and withdrawn nature, even though it has been tamed. Many people who like cats very much never seem to appreciate their need for independence and solitude, which is just as important for them as love and security. Nothing is more gentle than a loving cat trying to show its affection. But is must be the cat who initiates any display of feeling. The cat is an extraordinarily sensitive animal, and tolerates neither mediocrity nor excess, but prefers the delicate, shifting balance of a middle course.

The cat has been accused of hypocrisy. There are very few animals with such a highly developed mobility of expression, whose faces so clearly reflect the mood of the moment. The slightest nervous strain

The mother-cat has a whole variety of ways of talking to her kittens.

152

There is never any
doubt as to a cat's
meaning.

shows on a cat's face. When the ears are pricked back and the eyes wide open, the cat has a calm, confident, gentle face which can, however, change at the slightest emotion. You can see the change take place as the cat's face grows tense, the eyes turn to slits and the ears are laid back. A cat always gives warning before it attacks. Its whole attitude expresses what to expect, whether the adversary is human or animal. It gives an ultimatum, and its attack is generally defensive rather than aggressive.

The cat is certainly jealous, or, to be more exact, exclusive. One day, I brought a six-week-old puppy home. Until then, my cat had been the only animal in the house and when he saw me with the interloper he let out a fearful howl and disappeared, never to return. The howl was the kind of sound any man might make in the face of treachery. In man, such a cry is normally described as being like that of an animal, perhaps because it is spontaneous, and comes from the depths of our nature where we are at one with the animals in our instinctive hatred of disloyalty.

The cat seems to reserve its display of jealousy for its relationships with man. Once a cat has chosen an owner he places all his confidence in him, holds him in high esteem and cannot bear to see his idol fall. He is not so much upset by the sight of another animal as hurt by your concern for it. Your love is his alone and even at the best it takes some time for him to accept the idea of sharing.

CURIOSITY

Curiosity is inborn. The cat is fascinated by his surroundings—even the smallest happening makes him eager for fresh adventures. New ground has to be explored in minute detail and every object examined; parcels are sniffed, as if the cat were trying to guess the contents; an unknown visitor is examined from head to foot to find out what he may be thinking, and if the answer is satisfactory, will be approached.

Egyptian bronze of a kitten learning from his mother.

The cat likes to watch you working and to know what you are doing.

The cat uses all his agility to attain his ends and is intelligent enough invariably to find the easiest way.

HUNTING

The cat's innate intelligence and agility come into play when hunting. The hunting instinct brings out his affinity with the wild cat because the domestic cat is also a carnivore that hunts by stalking. Crouching behind a tuft of grass, or stretched alongside a tree, he lies in wait for his prey and watches. Then he creeps closer and closer, belly to the ground, unhurried, waiting. When he is near enough, the cat freezes, gently balancing his hindquarters to calculate his spring and, like a flash, falls on his victim, which he then devours with dagger-sharp teeth, holding it down with his claws.

Cats rarely miss. In the Middle Kingdom, Egyptians used to take cats hunting and fishing on the Nile marshes; neither the speed of the fish, nor the strong current, not even the sun's reflection off the water slowed down their lightning reactions.

SEXUAL BEHAVIOR

If the cat's inquisitive nature makes us compare it with women, what are we to say of its sexual behavior?

Aristotle assures us that 'female cats are much more temperamental than tom-cats and, far from repulsing them, they continuously provoke them without shame or circumspection, even chastising them.'

Then Buffon, the important French eighteenth-century naturalist, repeats the theme. 'Although it is rare in animals, the female cat seems more ardent than the male; she invites, searches and calls him, crying her desire, or rather the extremity of her need,

out loud; and if the male runs off or spurns her, she pursues him, biting and spitting, and forces him to satisfy her, although the actual mating is always painful.'

The tom-cat, a quiet unassuming animal in the ordinary way, is overwhelmed by his passionate nature when in season. He is a prey to violent excitement, and chaos reigns in his normally well-ordered

Two kittens playing together act out their future battles.

As nimble as a monkey, the cat can perform surprising feats of agility.

The cat can be the most affectionate of pets.

'Curiosity killed the cat,' goes the saying. Any novelty will soon be 'investigated.'

life: he cannot sleep, refuses food, forgets to wash and howls his wretchedness to the moon.

When the female is coming into season she will look for affection, come to be stroked, rub her head against you with much purring and sad eyes. In the next few days she will stretch out on her belly, roll about on her back and the purring will give way to a deeper, more raucous and ear-splitting call.

Then the tom-cat makes his appearance. Attracted by the female's calls, he comes to offer his services, and will pay court to her until the matter is settled. He is not the only one. Often three or four males join the queue for her favor, and it is at those times that the tom-cat loses his placid nature and is transformed into a warrior. Now it is no longer play, but real fighting, because only the one who succeeds in driving the others off will be able to claim the Beauty, who meanwhile watches the battle-scenes with an intense interest concealed behind feigned indifference.

The cat surveys the
scene from the
height of a tree,
never off his guard.

That is the behavior of single unattached cats, but
if you have a pair living together you will find that
they act like a human married couple. Aldous Huxley
said if one wanted to describe humans, one should
watch a pair of cats. The cat-pair knows all the joys,
miseries and jealousy of conjugal life. Watch the
female suspiciously sniffing her mate if he has been
out for a day or two, and the punishment she admin-
isters if she finds traces of another female! See the
repentant look of the unfaithful husband wait
humbly until the storm is over; then timidly start
licking her when he senses that she is considering
forgiveness!

The same ritual occurs if the female wanders, but
that rarely happens unless the male has been neutered.
In that case it is much better to have both cats altered,
so that they can live together in a state of Platonic
friendship.

MATERNAL AND PATERNAL INSTINCT

A mother-cat is so self-denying, so devoted and
loving with her kittens that she is the epitome of
mother-love.

From the first moment that she washes her new-
born kittens until their weaning and departure, she
is watchful, anxious at the slightest threat of danger
and attentive lest any of her kittens should stray or
get hurt. If the pair live together, the father will help
the mother protect and clean the kittens and will take
her place if she has to be away.

The tom-cat may have developed a paternal instinct
even if the female does not live with him. I once had
a cat that mated freely with a neighbor's female and
visited her two or three times a day. After greeting
one another, he would take her place with the young
while she went out. When she returned, he answered
all her anxious questions and then went off again,
leaving his family for several hours.

In the absence of the male, the cat will turn to you for help, even if it is only your presence that is required. When my cat is about to have her kittens, she refuses to leave me, and sits on my knee purring loudly. I can see her labour progressing. When I put her in the bed I have prepared for her, she likes me to stay, and stroke her gently, and if I take my hand away, she puts out a paw to draw it back. If I leave the room she gets up to follow. After the birth of the first kitten she can be left for a few minutes, because her instinct puts the kitten first, but if I am away too long she miaows to call me back. Then the look in her eyes is so full of love and absolute trust, so proud and serene, that it is difficult to understand how people can deny these animals a soul.

Fortunately we have progressed beyond Descartes and his theory that animals are mere machines which neither think nor feel, nor have the simplest form of conscious mentality. In his *Discours de la Méthode* Descartes advances two arguments in favor of this theory. The first is that animals do not talk, although some have speech organs; the second, that they possess a highly specialized instinct: he compares them with a clock 'made of springs and wheels' which can measure time better than man despite his intelligence, but can do nothing else.

Clearly instinct is partly mechanical, but is it right to insist on the mechanical side to the exclusion of all conscience? In opposition to Descartes, who was followed by Buffon and, more recently, by an American biologist, James Loeb, Etienne Condillac, the French eighteenth-century philosopher, finds it 'impossible to imagine that animals' reactions are purely mechanical.' He believes that 'animals make

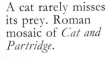
A cat rarely misses its prey. Roman mosaic of *Cat and Partridge*.

The Egyptians
used the cat to
retrieve their game.

comparisons and decisions, have ideas and a memory.'
And if their mental development is less advanced
than man's, it is simply that they do not need it, and
that their organism is capable of only rudimentary
language.

The cat is quite obviously intelligent, as one may
judge from the different forms of behavior described
above: its ability to make itself understood by other
cats and man, its methods of communicating, thinking and acting if faced with a problem, and of discri-
minating between different objects. The cat can certainly recognize cause and effect, for example in
Pola Weiss's story: 'A shop-cat used to sit on a bench
near the till, while the owners were upstairs. When
anyone came into the shop it pulled a bell-rope to
warn them.' Here the cat makes a double deduction:
first the connection between the stranger and the
bell, and secondly between the bell and the reap-
pearance of its owner. We are not told how it
happened in the first place. Was it voluntary? Did
the cat teach itself the trick? Research should be
directed toward finding out the origin of these apparently intelligent actions in cats, in order to establish

Concentration,
observation and
vigilance are part
of the cat's mental
equipment, all
necessary in the
hunting of rodents.

160

precise facts and discover how far the cat can prove
that its acts are intelligent and not merely association of ideas, by means of which its behavior appears,
to a certain point, intelligent.

Kant wrotes: 'To think is to reason.' Is the cat
capable of analytical thought, of making distinctions,
qualifying and synthesizing? In other words is it
capable of the concentration required in any intellectual exercise based on reason? Intelligence requires
attention, excludes distraction and presupposes vigilance, observation and interest in the subject. The
cat waiting beside a hole directs all its attention on

161

Wherever he is, whatever he is doing, the cat keeps his aura of mystery.

the emerging mouse; its vigilance is concentrated on a single objective.

Some animals quickly lose interest, are easily distracted, and consequently behave less intelligently. There may be varying levels of intelligence within the same species. Nor does the cat invariably escape this rule—as we know, no two cats are ever alike, and this does not make a study of their level of intelligence very easy. And indeed, are we ever going to be able to resolve this enigma, or will the cat always remain *Des grands sphinx allongés au fond des solitudes?*

STANDARD BREEDS

The breed, a subdivision of the species, is itself divided into varieties which combine common hereditary characteristics. With that official definition as our starting point, it must be admitted that there are few breeds, and their differences are relatively small compared with other domestic species.

The breeds of cat recognized by specialist societies (the G.C.C.F. or Governing Council of Cat Fancy and the F.E.F.E. or Fédération Internationale Féline d'Europe) show their distinctive characteristics to a differing extent—some can be called specific differences, while others are really nothing more than rather indefinite variations. Exact descriptions of the relative importance of breed characteristics enable us to assess how far specific zoological origin can be ascribed to any particular breed.

Siamese cats, for example, differ so strikingly from the European cat that it has been convincingly suggested that they have a different origin.

On the other hand the fact that the Manx cat has no tail should not be linked with its zoological origin. It is a mutation to be found in other species, including dogs, inhabiting the Isle of Man which leads one to think that the island itself is in some way responsible for this anomaly.

The Cat Societies, in an attempt to classify the different breeds and their varieties, have observed differences of conformation, shape and size, variations in the skin, the hair, or the pattern and coloring of the coat.

The breeds and varieties are generally natural. Some, however, have been modified by man after years of research and strict selection so that their characteristics are sufficiently hereditary and homogeneous to be capable of evolution. This gives them the right to be admitted to the 'holy of holies,' the selected breeds.

Serval *(Felis serval)*

It has been noticed that there is a connection between a white coat, blue eyes and deafness: white cats with blue eyes are deaf. It also has been observed that white kittens are deaf as long as their eyes remain blue; the deafness disappears later when the color of their eyes changes to orange.

White cats with odd eyes (one blue, one orange) generally have normal hearing, though deaf ones occasionally occur.

Breeding is based on selection: a kitten inherits half of its characteristics from each parent, a quarter from the grandparents and so on. Cat Clubs of England and the Continent have laid down the *Standard*, i.e. the characteristics needed to describe the theoretical type of every breed and variety. Every characteristic is classified with a certain number of points depending on its importance. The total—100—is perfection. The scale of points varies with the breed.

◀
Siamese and
European cat

European Tabby,
brown
▼

The evolution of an organism is conditioned by its genes, which are the basis of heredity. Like all other animals, genes are responsible for the cat's sex, morphology, coat color and eyes. Different breeds result from an alteration in one or more genes. If a gene mutates it reappears in a modified form. In a cross, where there are two opposing genes, the one which takes precedence, is called 'dominant,' the other 'recessive.' If, for example, you cross a black cat with a tabby one, the litter will nearly always be tabby. The tabby-coat is dominant over the black. All the coats appear in both male and female, except tortoiseshell, which is practically always female. Any male with this coloring will invariably be sterile.

THE EUROPEAN WILD CATS

The European wild cat *(felis sylvestris)*, is not the ancestor of our domestic cat—as was previously thought—but a completely different species, recognizable by its bone-structure as well as by its coat-pattern. It lives in hollow tree trunks, abandoned holes and crevices in the rocks. As a hunter it rivals man and is the enemy of all game.

GENERAL APPEARANCE

Body: Massive, bigger and heavier than the domestic cat. It weighs from five to eighteen kilograms and measures from $18\,^7/_{10}$ to $26\,^1/_2$ in. in length.
Head: Large, rounded. Relatively large, veined eye with a greenish-yellow iris.
Coat: Thick greyish-brown fur with a dark dorsal line; regular brown spots, redder on the belly, striped with black on body, legs and tail. Five black stripes radiate from the top of the head and fade away on the neck. The black color on the foot continues to the claws.
Tail: Relatively short, club-shaped, the fur thicker at the tip. It has seven to nine dark rings ending with black.
Ears: Pricked, black outside and yellowish inside.
History: The wild cat lives in northern and central Europe. It used to be very common in forests, but is now on the verge of extinction and can be found only in mountainous regions of Germany, the eastern Pyrenees, the Balkan mountains, and a few rare specimens in the Swiss Jura. It is also still encountered in Italy, England and Scotland, but is unknown either in Ireland or Scandinavia.

Long-tailed Siamese

Short-tailed Siamese

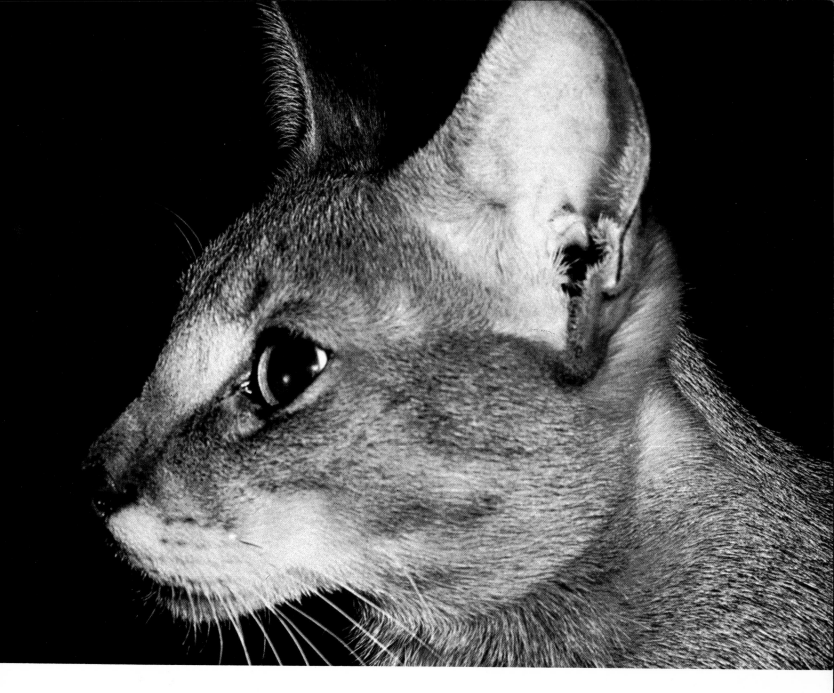

European wild cat ▶▶

Felis lybica ▶

European Tabby,
red

The wild cat is supposed to have appeared first in the form *Miacis* in the Eocene, the earliest Tertiary period and to have become established in the Miocene, the Upper Tertiary.

THE AFRICAN WILD CAT

The species of African cats varies so widely as to be rather confusing. In fact many of the species are actually only varieties, defined only by the color and pattern of the coat. The principal groups are: the golden cat *(felis aurata)*; the serval *(felis serval)*; the jungle cat *(felis chaus)* and the black-footed cat *(felis nigripes)*.

The most typical of all wild African cats is the tabby cat of which the sub-species, the 'gloved cat', is generally thought to be the ancestor of our domestic cat.

THE TABBY CAT (FELIS LIBYCA)

This cat is found everywhere in Africa from Algeria to the Cape and spreads into the Middle East, Syria and Arabia. This wide dispersal explains the great differences between specimens, which allow us to distinguish several sub-species, principally distinguished by color.

European Tiger-
tabby, brown

THE GLOVED CAT (FELIS LIBYCA MANICULATA)

This breed is classed officially now as *felis libyca Forster* or *felis ocreata gmelin*; in size it is very close to our domestic cat but the color and coat-pattern are different.

Coat: Tawny yellow or yellowish-grey, slightly redder behind the head and on the middle of the

Long-hair:
square-shaped head

European: round
head

Siamese:
wedge-shaped head

back; the flanks are lighter and the belly nearly white. The back has eight dark longitudinal stripes and the body has transverse stripes, becoming more distinct on the limbs. The body has a few black spots.

Tail: Tawny yellow with three black rings ending in a black tip.

Legs: Black horizontal stripes two thirds of the way up the leg; the foreleg and paws are gloved with a lighter color.

History: This cat lives in the wild in Nubia and Alfred Brehm, the German naturalist, believed that the domestic cat of the present Yemeni is of the same breed. Describing his last journey to Ethiopia he says: 'I have noticed that the domestic cat belonging to the people of the Yemen and to the Arabs on the west bank of the Red Sea are identical in color to the gloved cat and move with the same characteristic grace.'

The gloved cat was in all probability the one the Egyptians tamed because it can be recognized in the mummies and representations which have been preserved.

THE ASIAN WILD CAT

Some species are common to both Africa and Asia, as, for instance, the jungle cat and the golden cat; but the most important of the essentially Asiatic cats are the Manul and the Fishing Cat.

THE MANUL OR STEPPE CAT
(FELIS MANUL)

This is one of the largest and fiercest of the wild cats.
Body: Larger than the European wild cat with longer legs.
Head: Flecked with black and with two characteristic black stripes on the cheeks.
Coat: Very long coat, brownish-white flecked with brown hairs.
Tail: Long and tufted, ringed, with a black tip.
History: Still known as the Pallas Cat (the name of the person who discovered it), the Manul lives in the Asian steppe from Tibet to Amu-Darya.
Several authors believe this cat to be the ancestor of Angora or Persian cats because of the length and color of the coat, but these are quite secondary characteristics and the two types differ on much more essential points.

THE FISHING CAT OR TARAI
(FELIS VIVERRINA)

Unlike most cats, this one prefers a diet of fish, freshwater molluscs and large snakes, hence its name. It does, however, eat birds and mammals, and will attack dogs, sheep, young calves and even infants. It is a dangerous and powerful animal.
Body: Massive, about the same size as the European wild cat.
Head: For a cat it is close-set and narrow. The end of the nose is flesh-colored.
Coat: Coarse and dull. Its ground color is tawny grey, very varied, sometimes greyish, sometimes russet. The back has four rows of black spots which form stripes on the forehead. The cheeks are divided by three stripes, one continuing round the throat. Black behind the ears with a white spot. These spots are round on the flanks and horizontal on the legs.

History: The fishing cat lives in India, the southern Himalayas, Nepal and Assam, Tenasserim, Thailand, Ceylon and Formosa. Little is known of its habits in the wild, except that it prefers humid jungle on river banks, estuaries above the tidal zone, and swampy hunting ground.

DOMESTIC CATS

The classification of domestic breeds is usually quite arbitrary, according to the length and color of the coat and the country of origin. The different breeds of domestic cat vary little in conformation. The general shape of the head makes a good basis for classification, depending on whether it is round, triangular or square. The *European* cat has a round head with long ears, wide at the base, round eyes and a straight nose. *Siamese* and *Abyssinian* cats have a wedge-shaped head. In the case of the Siamese the upwards-slant of the eyes accentuates the triangular appearance. The *Persian* has a square head, its shape exaggerated by small, wide-set ears, round eyes and a small, short, flat nose.

The general morphology of the animal is also taken into account. Two different types of European cat can easily be distinguished: one is slim, elegant, strong and large; the other is frailer, smaller and stockier. Siamese cats are usually smaller than Europeans. Persians and Burmese are of medium or large size, but strong and stocky. These differences in conformation enable us to recognize two standard types: long and slim, short and cobby.

A theoretically perfect *Standard* has been agreed upon as a guide to breeders and to help judges actually doing the selection. Standards are not immutable. They can be modified, according to remarks made by breeders and judges. Sometimes differences of opinion can delay the setting of a new standard for many

White cat with
blue eyes ▶

White cat with odd
eyes ▶▶

◀ European Tabby,
silver

Detail of the
undercoat of the
European Smokes
▼

▲
Tortoiseshell

◀◀ European
Tortoiseshell

◀ European
Tiger-tabby, red

171

years, as happened in the dispute over the length of the Siamese cat's tail, which lasted nearly twenty years.

SHORT-HAIRS

The short-hair is divided into two classes: European and foreign. European cats comprise the European breed proper, the British Blue (Chartreuse), and the Manx Cat.

I EUROPEAN SHORT-HAIR

The cat known as European is the ordinary domestic, short-haired variegated cat, man's pet, not only in Europe but throughout the world. It is the most common and best-known breed in town and country. Although fine specimens do appear, its breeding is often haphazard, making it difficult to fix the type. The cat is a good size, sturdy and well-formed with a broad chest and a well-furnished tail, wide at the base,

European Spotted

strong and long in proportion to the body. European cats are classified as follows: selfs, tri-colors, tabby, striped and bi-colors plus a few rare specimens called 'smoke' (dark with a white undercoat).

1. THE EUROPEAN TABBY

The tabby coat is infinitely varied but a very clear, symmetrical coat pattern is typical.

Standard	
Color	Warm and glossy. Three dark stripes run down the spine as far as the base of the tail. Legs and tail are ringed with stripes. The head should not have light parts; the stripes converging on the nose should form regular stripes on the cheeks. The chest carries two black horizontal stripes with a third at the base of the neck. Oval markings on the shoulders form a butterfly pattern with the feet when the standing animal is seen from above. The pattern on the flanks resembles an oyster-shell. White on the chest or a white belly are faults. The European tabby is divided into three colors: *Red Tabby:* Red with warm red markings. *Silver Tabby:* Silver-grey with dark blue-grey markings. *Brown Tabby:* Fawn with dark brown markings. The most common variety. The kittens are not clearly marked until they reach six months old.
Body	Sturdy, long.
Head	Fine and wedge-shaped, flat cheeks.
Eyes	Round. Green in the Silver Tabby; yellow, amber or green in the Brown Tabby; and orange or amber in the Red Tabby.
Coat	Very dense and glossy.
Scale of show points	Color and markings: 25 — body: 25 — head: 25 — eyes: 10 — coat: 15. Total: 100.

History: This is the most common of all cats. It is well adapted to town and country life. The brown tabby is closest to the wild animal and the clarity of his markings gives him a remarkable appearance, he looks like a wild animal in miniature. However, the lateral stripes characteristic of his coat are not found on any wild cat.

2. EUROPEAN TIGER-STRIPE

This cat should be clearly distinguished from the tabby. His name describes his coat which resembles the tiger.

Standard

Color	The markings are well-defined but slightly smudged. The stripes run from the spine down the flanks underneath the belly. Legs and tail are ringed. Colors are the same as the tabby: red, silver and brown.
Body	Short and stocky. The neck is short, close up to the head. Shoulders are broad.
Head	Massive with broad cheeks.
Eyes	Round. Green or hazel in the Silver Tiger-Stripe, orange or copper color in the Red and Brown Tiger-Stripe.
Coat	Glossy and dense.

Scale of show points   Coat pattern and color: 25 — body: 25 — head: 25 — eyes: 10 — coat: 15. Total: 100.

History: Cross-breading has so altered the genetic evolution of European cats that it is very difficult to isolate pure-bred individuals. Many of the cats classed as *Tiger-Tabbies* are no more than ordinary tabbies with a poor coat pattern. This cat comes nearest to the European wild cat in its markings and will adapt easily to the wild. In fact the tiger-tabby comprises the greater number of domestic cats living wild, and is often erroneously called a wild cat. The difference between them is easily seen by looking at the tail: the wild cat has a short, tufted tail, while the domestic animal gone wild has a large tail marked with regular rings.

3. THE SPOTTED EUROPEAN CAT

This cat is neither tabby nor striped and its most important point is that the spots should be very distinct. They may be small and numerous or large and sparse.

Standard

Color	The spots must be very clear and distinct, blending in with the ground color. Stripes are admissible only on the face and head.
Body	Rather long and powerful.
Head	Delicate without exaggerated cheeks.
Eyes	Eyes match the color of the coat.
Coat	Glossy and dense.
Scale of show points	Color (spots): 50 — body: 10 — head: 15 — eyes: 15 — coat: 10. Total: 100.

History: This cat was exhibited for the first time in 1880. Its coat-pattern is one of the oldest known among English cats. The variety is gaining ground on the show bench.

4. EUROPEAN TRI-COLOR

The coat-pattern is three colored and the two varieties are distinguished, on the basis of the color arrangement—tortoiseshell and tortoiseshell and white.

a) *European Tri-Color (Tortoiseshell)*
This is the English 'tortie' so called because its coat resembles a tortoiseshell. Although the coat apparently has only two colours it is actually composed of light touches of black, red and cream in a random mixture with no stripes. There should be a red blaze on the face.

b) *European Tri-Color (Tortoiseshell and White)*
This coat-pattern is black, red and cream with the addition of white. The white is often dominant, but the colors should be evenly balanced. An all-white paw or chest constitutes a defect, but a red blaze on the face is good.

Standard

Color	Color is most important: the colors and pattern should be distinct and evenly distributed especially on the face.
Body	Well muscled, long legs but with a delicate, small bone-structure.
Head	Delicate, round, straight nose, round eyes.
Eyes	Green, orange or copper, very round.
Coat	Glossy and soft.
Scale of show points	Color: 50 — body: 20 — head: 10 — eyes: 10 — coat: 10. Total: 100.

History: With a few rare exceptions tri-colored cats are female. If one finds a tri-colored male he will be sterile. Geneticists explain this characteristic as an interaction between genes which determines the cream and black in the coat. The genes are carried by an X chromosome. If the male has only one X chromosome which produces either black or cream, then the coat will be self-colored. The female, however, has two X chromosomes. Each chromosome may have a gene of a different color, black or cream, in which case the two genes alternate producing the tortoiseshell coat. This kind of female can produce black or cream males but the females will be either the color of the father or tortoiseshell. The tortoiseshell and white variety is very common near the Franco-Spanish frontier, hence its French name— 'Spanish Cat.'

5. EUROPEAN BI-COLOR (MAGPIE)

a) *European Pied*
This cat is usually black and white, although the description is applied to any cat with large patches of color on a white ground: red and white, or grey and white, for instance. Although an even distribution of the patches and white whiskers make a handsome animal, the standard has recently been revised for exhibition.

Standard

Color	Any solid color with white. The patches of color should be distinct and evenly distributed. Not

more than two thirds color and not more than half white. The color on the face should also be divided by a white blaze on the nose.

Body	Cobby and powerful.
Head	Large and round; neat, well-pricked ears set wide apart. Small nose, large cheeks, broad muzzle.
Eyes	Large and round, set well apart, deep orange, yellow or copper.
Coat	Short, fine texture.
Tail	Short and powerful.
Scale of show points	Color: 25 — body: 15 — head: 25 — eyes: 15 — coat: 15 — tail: 5. Total: 100.

b) *European Smoke*

A black or very dark tiger-stripe with a silver under-coat. The undercoat only appears when the cat matures, that is when the kittens are six to seven months old. Unlike the Smokey Persian, this type breeds true from father to son, although originally it must have been only the result of an odd cross. Unlike the Smoke Long-Hairs, the Europeans do not have a light-colored ruff, but the blacks have the same copper eyes and the Tiger-Stripes, green eyes. Their breeding is still in the experimental stage.

Standard (Provisional)

Color	Black or tiger-striped black with a silvery white undercoat and sharp contrast.
Body	Firm and muscular, well-formed and powerful. Broad, strong chest, well-proportioned legs.

European white

Head	Round and broad with small ears, slightly rounded at the tip, narrow at the base.
Eyes	Copper or green (black, smoke, tiger-stripe).
Coat	Short, fine, dense.
Tail	Thick at the base, well placed and fairly long.
Scale of show points	Color: 40 — body: 15 — head: 15 — coat: 15 — eyes: 5 — tail: 10. Total: 100.

6. EUROPEAN SELF

This is one of the most common of cats, although true specimens of one color are rare. A fine, slender cat with long legs and a thin neck. Four colors are accepted: white, black, cream and red.

a) *White Self*

Coat: The coat should be unblemished with no sign of yellow, grey or any other color.

Eyes: Blue, orange or yellow, but rarely green.

History: White cats with blue eyes are the most sought after even though they are usually born deaf, presenting a great obstacle to communication. They are also very difficult to rear.

b) *Black Self*

Coat: It should be jet black and glossy, free from white and mixtures of grey and brown, and it should not have a russety tone. Even one or two white hairs constitute a defect.

Eyes: Very pure in color, yellow, orange or copper, but never green. The finest specimens have almond-shaped eyes in a snake-like head.

History: A very popular cat. A symbol of good or bad luck, depending on one's point of view.

c) *Cream Self*

Coat: The coat should be cream and show no trace of stripes or white marking.

Eyes: Copper or hazel.

History: Perfect specimens are very rare.

European Self, black

d) *Red Self*

Coat: The color should be very dark, tawny red, without stripes or markings. It is very rare and has apparently never been selected for a specific breeding program.

Standard for all Selfs

Body	Long, slim legs, long, thin, glossy tail.
Head	Held high on a long neck. Rectangular nose, straight muzzle (more delicate in the whites), large ears.
Eyes	Round, except in the blacks, when they are slightly slanting. Color variable depending on variety.
Coat	Velvety and dense. Not coarse.
Color	No spots or markings.
Scale of show points	Body and size: 30 — eyes: 10 — color: 10 — head: 30 — coat: 10 — tail: 10. Total: 100.

II British Blue (Chartreuse)

This is one of the oldest Continental breeds which was already known to Buffon. It makes a powerful impression. It is sweet-natured, affectionate and intelligent and adapts well to changes of temperature, because its thick coat protects it from cold and damp. It is an excellent rat-catcher.

Standard

Body	Solid and heavy on long, muscular legs. The neck is powerful and the chest round and low. The belly has very thick fur.
Head	The head is round and rather broad at the base. Strong jaw with blue, almost black lips. The bulbous nose is a silvery grey, dark or light in tone depending on the coat. Medium-sized ears, set high on a very round skull. Full cheeks.
Eyes	Yellow or orange. The fine dark gold color gives the face a very sweet expression.
Color	The palest to the darkest grey tones are allowed. The most popular color is a fine, pale greyish blue. No shading or marking is allowed. White hairs are defects. Kittens sometimes retain their dark stripes for several months but these stripes should disappear as the animal matures.
Coat	The hair is woolly and dense and feels very much like an otter.
Tail	Very slim, long and jaunty. One of the characteristics of this type. NB. Any compromise between the British and the Russian Blue should be eliminated.
Scale of show points	Body and size: 25 — head: 25 — eyes: 10 — coat: 10 — color: 20 — tail: 10. Total: 100.

History. Tradition has it that this cat originally came from South Africa and was brought to France by Carthusian monks. Most authorities believe it to be the result of a cross between an Egyptian and Manul cat. For some years now it has been very carefully bred thanks to the efforts of the British Blue Cat Club, which is trying to eliminate the confusion between the blues.

III The Manx Cat

This cat is remarkable for its lack of a tail. Its coat-color is like other European cats, but its conformation is noticeably different. The hind-quarters are carried very high, the back is short with broad flanks, which gives it a leaping gait, rather like that of a rabbit. It is a good ratter, faithful, intelligent and affectionate.

Standard

Tail	Must be lacking. There should be a hollow or depression where one would normally expect a tail. Nevertheless in otherwise very fine specimens a small bunch of hair on the final cartilage of the spinal column is permitted.
Hind-quarters	There should be considerable difference in the height of the front and back legs, which cannot be too tall, since they control the jumping gait so characteristic of this cat.
Conformation of the spine	Short. This cat is very cobby.
Crupper	Well developed, absolutely round with deep flanks.
Coat	The fur is short and fine like a rabbit's, with a soft, thick undercoat.

British Blue (Chartreuse)

178

Head	The same as the European cat.
Coat Color and pattern	Self, tabby or tiger-stripe like the European cat.
Eyes	The color is of secondary importance and is the same as any European cat having the same coat: blue for the white cats, yellow or orange for the blacks, copper or hazel for tigers, tabbies and so on.
Scale of show points	Tail (lack of): 15 — hind-quarters: 15 — back: 15 — crupper: 10 — flanks: 10 — fur: 10 — head: 10 — color: 5 — eyes: 5 — condition: 5. Total: 100.

History: Cats without tails are found in several parts of the world. They are sometimes depicted in Japanese of Chinese prints. In Europe they are confined to the Isle of Man, hence the name.

It is possible that these cats were imported from the Far East and left on the island by Spanish sailors at the time of the Armada. It is more likely however that they are the result of a mutation arising from the fact that they inhabit an island, since there are also tail-less dogs on the Isle of Man. Such an anomaly might have arisen from conditions peculiar to the island. In any case, imported or autochthonous, the cats are undoubtedly a specific breed.

II FOREIGN SHORT-HAIR

These cats are long, graceful and supple. The head is long and wedge-shaped with a large skull and narrow muzzle. The eyes are almond-shaped, the ears large, broad at the base and pointed at the tips. The tail is long, thin, tapering and very flexible.

1. ABYSSINIAN

This breed is the closest to the cats worshipped by the ancient Egyptians. It looks like a wild cat but is not so fierce, and is, in fact, docile and timid by nature. It is slow to make friends but can be very affectionate. It needs plenty of space since it does not thrive in a small run. It is very lively, somewhat unruly even, playing like a kitten until quite an advanced age. This very delicate cat is also the most carnivorous.

Standard

Body	Medium-sized, rather small and slender. This cat holds his pretty and expressive head high, and has a proud, elegant appearance.
Head	Delicate, wedge-shaped with large, pointed ears, broad at the base.
Eyes	Very expressive, large and round. Green, hazel or yellow.
Tail	Long and well-furnished, slightly pointed.
Legs and Paws	The legs are fine-boned, ending in small blackish feet. This black continues around the back of the hind feet.
Color	Color plays a great part in the handsome appearance of this cat. It resembles the European hare, but the undercoat should be ruddy, not grey. The best color is a warm, golden brown, uniform without being dull, and showing neither spots nor stripes. White on the neck is a significant defect. Typical of the breed is the ticked coat—each hair, tawny for three quarters of its length, ends with a double or triple black bar; the ticking covers head, back, and tail, while the chest and belly are tawny. There is also an *Abyssinian Red*, differing from the Abyssinian only in the color of the hair which is a reddish copper color with a double or triple band of darker red at the tip of the hair.

Scale of show points: Color of the body: 30 — color of the ticking: 20 — conformation: 20 — head and ears: 15 — eyes: 5 — condition: 10. Total: 100.

History: Imported into England from Africa in 1869 the cat is unknown in Ethiopia. It was described for the first time in 1874 by Dr. Gordon Stables in his book *Cats, Their Points and Characteristics.* Since the foundation of the Abyssinian Cat Club in England in 1926, the breed has been developed and great efforts made to improve it.

2. SIAMESE

The Siamese cat is a short-haired cat with unique characteristics of color and conformation. It differs from our domestic cats to such a marked degree that some people maintain that it has a completely different origin. It is true that Siamese and ordinary cats do not get on well together, even showing a distinct aversion to each other.

The Siamese cat has a singular cry, but its most important characteristic is its ovarian cycle, which differs from the European breed. Siamese cats come into season throughout the year. The season lasts eight to ten days with intervals of twelve days, while the European cat is in heat only two or three times a year for four to six days. The gestation period is sixty-five to sixty-eight days for the Siamese against sixty-two to sixty-four for the European. The kittens are ash-white at birth, and the blue or brown marks only appear later.

Another characteristic is the tail. Siamese enthusiasts have disagreed about the tail. Formerly a broken, knotted or atrophied tail was thought essential for the pure-breeds; but now it appears that the short-tailed cats come not from Thailand, but from Vietnam where they interbred with common short-tailed cats from Indonesia.

Thus the true Siamese has a long tail.

Siamese cats are classified by color.

a) *Seal-Point*

This is the classic type of Siamese, pale fawn in color with seal-brown mask, feet, ears and tail.

b) *Blue-Point*

The typical dark markings are bluish-grey instead of brown. The coat is generally a glacial white, blending perfectly with the blue. This cat is reminiscent of Copenhagen porcelain.

c) *Chocolate-Point*

The markings are of a lighter brown, like milk chocolate. The coat is ivory white.

d) *Lilac-Point*

This popular but rather strange coloring is very difficult to achieve. It results from crossing blue and chocolate-point Siamese. It has a longer muzzle than the classical Siamese.

e) *Tabby-Point* (Lynx-Point)

This type differs from other Siamese by having silvery stripes instead of the usual colors. The body is pale cream and free of markings. Its graceful appearance has won it many admirers and the kittens are much in demand.

f) *Red-Point*

The ears, mask, paws and tail are a good reddish gold and the eyes a luminous blue. The coat is white, sometimes with delicate apricot shading. Unlike other Siamese, the stripes or markings on the extremities are not considered to be a defect. This is a very new variety.

g) *Tortie-Point*

This variety has only just been recognized. The body is cream, shading gradually into a warmer color on the back. The markings are brown and red, or chocolate and red, evenly distributed, distinct and glossy. There is no white. The Siamese tortie is invariably female, like all cats of this variety whatever the species.

General Standard for Siamese

Body	Medium-sized, long and slim, on delicate legs. The hind legs are slightly longer than the front, the feet are small and oval, the tail long and shaped like a whip-lash. A slightly-hooked tail of normal length is permitted.
Head	Large, well-proportioned and wedge-shaped, broad across the eyes, narrowing down to the muzzle. The ears are set fairly close, large, broad at the base and pointed.
Eyes	Wide set, large, pure in color and lustrous, they slant toward the nose, thus accentuating their oriental shape. They are intense blue in color. Squinting is a defect.
Color and markings	The general color of the coat varies through tones of cream, depending on variety, becoming paler until it is almost white under the belly. The ends of the paws, legs, the mask and the tail should be seal-brown, blue, lilac, chocolate, red or marked, depending on variety. Kittens are quite pale without marking.
Coat	Very short, fine-textured, smooth and glossy.
Scale of show points	a) *Type and conformation:* head: 15 — ears: 15 — eyes: 5 — body: 15 — legs and paws: 5 — tail: 5 = 50; b) *Color:* eyes: 15 — marking: 10 — body: 10 = 35; coat texture: 10 — condition: 5. Total: 100.

History: Although the true origin of the Siamese cat remains the secret of the jungles of Asia, the history of its introduction into Europe is well-known. The first pair was imported from Bangkok into England by Owen Gould in 1884. They were named Pho and Mia and their offspring carried off the first prizes in the Crystal Palace Exhibition of 1885. Until that time, these cats had been jealously guarded in the Royal Palaces in Siam (now Thailand). To steal a single one was a sacrilege, punishable by death. Despite this risk, several kittens were stolen and sold to naval officers travelling to Shanghai, but they rarely reached Europe.

Again in 1885 another pair, Tian O'Shian and Susan, belonging to Miss Forestier-Walker, were brought to England, and according to the Siamese

Cat Register of England, fifty per cent of all Siamese cats in the country today are their descendants.

The same year, the French Resident Minister in Siam, Auguste Pavie, sent a couple to the Jardin des Plantes in Paris. Professor Oustalet of the Paris Museum made the first scientific report on these cats in the *Magasin Pittoresque* of 1893. His description of the cats corresponds to the type we know: 'The tail is slender and cylindrical,' thus confirming the decision which settled the dispute over 'the tail question.' The imported adults soon became acclimatized but the kittens proved difficult to rear, probably because they were too coddled, and kept in unnatural surroundings; the Siamese cat needs space, and an apartment is not the best environment.

3. BURMESE

Four colors are distinguished: Burmese Brown or Sable, Blue, Cream and Blue-Cream. These are short-haired cats remarkable for the uniform color of the coat.

a) *Burmese Brown*
This cat is still known as Sable, from its coat-coloring, but it resembles a Siamese with its uniform brown coat and lack of variation in tone between the body and the extremities. The kittens are dark brown at birth. The cat should not be fat, but muscular. Its voice is similar to that of the Siamese.

b) *Burmese Blue*
This type differs from the Brown only in its color. The dominant color is a bluish-grey, slightly darker on the back. The general impression is very warm with silver overtones. The tail should be dark bluish-grey like the back, with no white or stripes.

c) *Burmese Cream*
This is a very rich color becoming lighter on the chest and belly. It should have no spots or stripes. In an otherwise excellent cat, slight shading is permitted. The ears are a little darker than the back. The kittens are lighter in tone, but should not have white spots.

d) *Burmese Blue-Cream*
The blue and cream color should be well mixed without stripes. But color and marking are less important than the type, which must be excellent because the Blue-Cream is in between the Brown-Blues and the Red-Creams.

The standard is similar to other Burmese but the scale of points is different.

Scale of show points	Color: 15 — body: 30 — head: 20 — eyes: 15 — coat: 10 — condition: 10. Total: 100.

General Standard for Burmese

Body	Medium-sized, fine and slim. The neck is long, legs slim, the back legs longer than the front, lifting the hind-quarters. The paws are oval and small, the tail thin and very tapered.
Head	Short and wedge-shaped, broad between the eyes. The pointed ears are fairly big and broad at the base.
Eyes	Almond-shaped and sloping, with no trace of squint. They should be yellow or copper, never green and especially not blue.
Color	In the Brown, Blue, Cream and Blue-Cream Burmese the color is very good, fading slightly down the breast and belly, with no markings of any kind. The mask and marks on the tail, ears and paws are slightly darker. The mask is joined to the ears by a dark line.
Coat	Short, glossy, silky, dense and smooth.
Scale of show points	Body: 25 — head: 15 — eyes: 15 — coat: 10 — color: 25 — condition: 10. Total: 100.

History: In 1930 Dr. G. C. Thomson of San Francisco imported a Burmese cat into the U.S.A. It had a short dark brown coat, paws with no glove markings and yellow eyes. It did not resemble the sacred Burmese cat and was thought to be a variety of Siamese. However, an American officer who had

Siamese, Lilac-point ▶

◀ Siamese,
Chocolate-point

▲
Burmese, Brown

▲
Siamese, Red-point

Chestnut brown ▶
(Havana)

◀ Russian, blue

Abyssinian, ruddy
▶

◀ Siamese, Blue-point

spent a long time in Burma declared that he had seen similar cats in temples at Mandalay. Whether or not it is a Siamese hybrid or a true species, the Burmese cat has been recognized since 1954 by The Governing Council of the Cat Fancy.

4. RUSSIAN BLUE

This cat is sometimes called the American or Maltese and it is often confused with the Chartreuse. However, unlike the Chartreuse, the Russian cat is slim and elegant like the cat of ancient Egypt. Fine lines, light conformation and a long face and neck give it a very feline appearance. It is a good rat-catcher although its build is a slight disadvantage. It is a very affectionate animal.

Standard

Body	Long, graceful, standing tall, thin legs, well-rounded paws, fine, flexible, slightly curved neck.
Tail	Long and thin, absolutely smooth. A standard tail is essential.
Head	Held high, wedge-shaped with a flat narrow skull, sloping forehead and long muzzle with no break between.
Eyes	Wide set and almond-shaped, fine pale, or emerald, green.
Ears	Fairly large, broad at the base narrowing to points with very little fur inside. The skin should be thin and transparent with little hair.
Hair	Short and thick, rather smooth and glossy like mink.
Color	Uniform, greyish-blue without overtones or markings. All shades of blue are admissible, from medium to dark.
Scale of show points	Conformation and size: 30 — head: 30 — eyes: 10 — coat: 10 — color: 10 — tail: 10. Total: 100.

History: Despite its name, this cat did not probably originate in Russia, and in fact nothing is definitely known of its origin. Common in England, Scandinavia and the U.S.A., it is said to have been imported into England by sailors on ships trading between England and Archangel.

Hairless Cat
(Sphynx)

186

5. HAVANA (OR CHESTNUT)

This color is also known in Europe as Chestnut. It differs from the Brown Burmese in its conformation: the Burmese is broader and more compact whereas the Havana is more like the Russian Blue. It is supple and sinuous with graceful proportions. The uniform mahogany of its coat is noticeably warmer in tone than that of the Burmese.

Standard

Body	Long, flexible, and muscular. Graceful shape with slender legs, the hind-quarters slightly taller. The paws are oval with pink pads.
Head	The head is long and well-proportioned with a narrow muzzle. The ears are big, broad at the base and set wide apart. The whiskers and nose are the same color as the coat.
Coat	The coat is short and glossy in a more or less dark mahogany, uniform overall.
Tail	Long, slender, without twists.

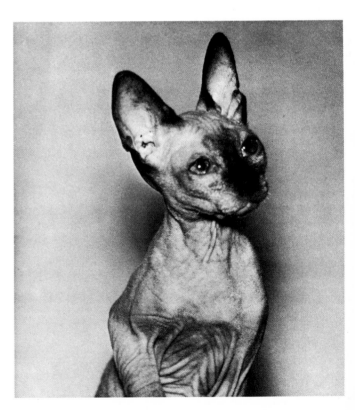

Cornish Rex (curly coat) and Devon Rex

Eyes   Oriental, slanting towards the nose, pure green in color.

Scale of   Body: 30 — head: 15 — coat: 30 — tail: 5 —
show points   eyes: 10 — condition: 10. Total: 100.

History: The Havana or Chestnut was bred in Great Britain from an accidental cross between a female Black Long-Hair and a male Chocolate-Point Siamese. From this litter a black female kitten was re-crossed with a Siamese and one of that litter had the Chocolate-Point Siamese gene: it was a male Chestnut Self. The Chestnut had arrived.

6. THE HAIRLESS CAT

The hairless cat, chilly, thin and unaesthetic, is not very popular with cat-lovers and seems to have little interest other than as a zoological freak. It was produced by Professor Létard in the Ecole Vétéri-naire at Alfort in France and there are a few specimens in America and Europe. Perhaps their origin should be sought in the 'Skinned Cats' of Mexico, a breed which is believed to be virtually extinct. The skinned cat does have some fur but it is very short. Its back is sable while the neck and the belly are pinkish. Also the kittens are born with a very thin fur and fine undercoat. After weaning this embryonic coat falls and the adult is completely smooth.

The hairless factor has been studied more among other domestic animals, especially the dog, but also the pig, goat, horse and cattle. Genetic research has shown that the genetic hairless character is negative, controlling a weakness that prevents breeding from a pair of these cats. One of the parents has to be normal. Hence there is no pure race of bald cats.

Hairless cats are not found on sale because they are really only a curiosity and no attempt has been made to breed them.

7. THE REX

This cat was called Rex because its coat is similar to that of the Astrex rabbit. It is absolutely curly, much shorter than that of other short-haired cats and has a soft feel like a broadtail lamb.

The Fédération Internationale Féline d'Europe recognizes two varieties of Rex-coated cat: The Cornish Rex, Gene I, and the Devon Rex, Gene II.

a) *Cornish Rex*

Standard

Coat	Thick, very short and soft, waving or rippling. It covers the whole body except the head and the paws. Whiskers and eyebrows should also be wavy. All colors are acceptable.
Head	Medium wedge with a flat skull, and, seen in profile, a straight line should run from the centre of the forehead to the end of the nose. The ears should be big and broad at the base, set high on the head.
Eyes	Oval-shaped, medium size conforming in color to the coat.
Body	Slender and muscular, of medium size with long, delicate legs making the cat seem very tall.
Tail	Long, fine and tapering.
Scale of show points	Coat: 50 — head: 15 — eyes: 5 — body: 25 — tail: 5. Total: 100.

b) *Devon Rex*

Standard

Coat	Short, fine, rippling coat, less curly than the Cornish Rex. The whole body is covered except the head and paws. The whiskers and eyebrows are stumped rather than wavy. All colors are accepted.
Head	The head is wedge-shaped with full cheeks and broad-set eyes. The muzzle is short with a strongly marked stop, and the forehead curves back to a flat skull. Ears are large, set rather low and far apart, with rounded tips.
Eyes	Fairly large, almond-shaped, the outer corner in a line with the ears. They conform to the coat color.
Body	Long and slender, well muscled and of average size. Legs should be long and slim, emphasizing the height. Paws are small and oval. A slim neck.
Tail	Fine, long and tapering.

History: The first ripple-coated cats appeared in 1950 in the West of England. That was the breed called Cornish Rex. Ten years later the Devon Rex appeared. They were first exhibited at the 37th International Exhibition in Paris. Any breed of cat can be produced with a Rex coat. Geneticists think that this mutation has only one recessive factor. Now recognized as a breed in its own right, this type of cat is becoming more and more popular because, apart from its unusual appearance, it is intelligent, affectionate and playful.

LONG-HAIRS

For many years Long-Haired cats were classified as either Persian or Angora. In England specialists now prefer the name Long-Hair, with sub-division into varieties. There are great differences in colour, but the standard of every breed requires that the coat should be full, silky, glossy and flowing.

Black Long-hair

188

The cat originated in Ankara and English breeders have developed the powerful carriage of this cobby type by interbreeding. It is a really beautiful pet, but can still be a good rat-catcher on occasion.

Apart from the standard (formerly Persian), other Long-Hairs are the Turkish Cat, the Cameo Tortoiseshell, the Maine Coon, the Himalayan Cat and the sacred Burmese Cat.

Long-Hairs exist in several distinct colors, each classified as a variety with its own particular standard. However they all conform to a general type. The Long-Haired cat's eyes are very different from those of the European or Siamese cat. They are larger and rounder; the slanting eyes demanded by the Siamese and accepted in the European are never acceptable in the Long-Hair. The eyes must also be wide open. Color of the eyes is very variable, ranging from orange to copper, intense blue or green; but it is always very pure. Slight veining or suggestion of any other color will eliminate an otherwise perfect specimen.

Detractors of the Long-Haired cat complain that it is lazy, sly, obstinate, unintelligent and vain, giving their dislike free rein. These defects may, certainly, apply to some Long-Hairs, but it is wrong to condemn the whole breed on that account. The Long-Hair often has a gentle, quiet nature with considerable charm.

The Long-Haired cat was first introduced about 1550 into Italy by a certain Pietro della Valle, and from there into France by Councillor Peresc of the Parliament of Aix-en-Provence. It probably originated in the Middle East. Some breeders make a clear distinction between the Persian Long-Hair and the Angora Long-Hair, seeing the latter as the result of a cross between a Persian and an ordinary cat. It is more likely that the Persians were descendants of the Angoras, carefully selected to develop their stocky appearance.

Blue Long-hair

1. BLACK LONG-HAIR

Cats of this type are very difficult to find, and absolutely black specimens with copper red eyes are rare and much sought after. It is difficult to know whether the new-born kitten will develop into a perfect adult specimen; sometimes their coats are brownish or grey until they mature.

The Long-Hairs need special preparation for showing. They must be carefully combed and kept out of the sun because it gives a rusty appearance to the coat. A few days before the show the coat should be wiped with a flannel wrung out in a very diluted mixture of ammonia and tepid water. Then it can be polished with a dry cloth.

Standard
Color   Glossy black to the roots, with no trace of brown, white or other marking.

Coat	Long and silky with a well-furnished ruff and tail.
Body	Cobby and massive on large short legs.
Head	Round and broad with small ears set wide apart and well-covered with fur. Full cheeks, broad muzzle and accentuated chin.
Eyes	Large, wide-open, deep orange in color. Very pure. No green rim is allowed.
Scale of show points	Color: 25 — coat: 20 — body: 20 — head: 20 — eyes: 15. Total: 100.

History: The Black was one of the first Long-Haired cats to be shown in Europe. Breeders have tried to improve the conformation of the Blacks by crossing with the Blues; an excellent dark blue female Long-Hair should be mated with a very fine Black. Only the females are kept for breeding and both Blue and Black are mated with Black. The second generation also mated with a Black Long-Hair will produce a large proportion of fine colored Blacks, of excellent type and eyes of good color. Several champions have been produced in this way.

2. WHITE LONG-HAIR

The Fédération Internationale Féline of Europe recognizes two types of White Long-Hair: the White with blue eyes and the White with orange eyes. The Americans also recognize the White with odd eyes, one blue and one orange.

Sometimes the kittens are born with a small shady black spot between the ears. It will disappear completely in a few weeks.

Looking after these animals requires time and patience. They should be brushed and combed frequently, using a white powder. But if they are to be shown all traces of powder must be removed or they will be disqualified.

a) *White (Blue Eyes)*

White Long-Hairs with blue eyes are always deaf. Biologists explain this by a genetic link between the blue eyes, the white coat and deafness. However, careful selection has sometimes enabled breeders to eliminate the fault.

Standard	
Color	Pure white with no mark or shading.
Coat	Long, silky and flowing. Well furnished ruff and tail. The hair should be supple and dense.
Body	Cobby without being too heavy, standing low on the feet with strong bone-structure.
Head	Round and wide with small eyes set far apart. A well-defined short nose, full cheeks and broad muzzle.
Eyes	Large and round, wide open. Blue sapphire color.
Scale of show points	Color: 25 — coat: 20 — body: 20 — head: 20 — eyes: 15. Total: 100.

History: The White Long-Hair is the direct descendant of the ancient White Angora of Asia Minor which was the pet of the harems in Istanbul. The first specimens to be imported had blue eyes. They are the basic type.

b) *White (Orange Eyes)*

This variety is more common than the Blue-Eyed White and is becoming very popular, probably because the Orange-Eyed Long-Hair is not deaf.

Standard	
Color	Very pure white, with no shading or marking.
Coat	Very silky and full with a well-furnished ruff and tail. The coat should be very fluffy, not woolly.
Body	Cobby, massive without being heavy, strongly boned and low on the legs.
Head	Round and wide with small ears set wide apart. Short nose, full cheeks and wide muzzle.
Eyes	Round, large and wide open, of a deep orange color. Small eyes are a defect.
Scale of show points	Color: 25 — coat: 20 — head: 20 — eyes: 15 — body: 20. Total: 100.

History: Whites with Orange Eyes have been recognized as a distinct breed since 1938. The two varieties are judged separately in shows, because otherwise the Long-Hair with Orange Eyes, being a purer breed than the Blue-Eyed White, carries off all the prizes.

◄ Long-hair, Red
Tabby

Long-hair,
Tortoiseshell blue
and white
▼

▲
Long-hair,
Silver-tabby

Long-hair,   ►
Tortoiseshell

Long-hair, Brown
colourpoint and
Long-hair, Blue
colourpoint   ►►

Birman, Blue
point and Birman,
Seal point   ►►

199

Scale of   Color: 10 — coat: 15 — head: 25 — shape of
show points   eyes: 10 — color of eyes: 10 — body: 10 —
             tail: 10 — condition: 10. Total: 100.

History: The Colorpoint Long-Hair (called the Himalayan in the United States) is one of the latest products of English breeders. This variety was not recognized in England till 1955, but its popularity is increasing. In fact breeders everywhere had been trying for a long time to produce a Siamese with long hair, but the elegance of the Siamese did not suit its new long coat. In successive crossings breeders have tried to eliminate the Siamese body conformation and to retain only the colors. They have succeeded in producing the Colorpoint Long-Hair, which resembles the Siamese only in the color of its coat and eyes.

12. CAMEO (LONG-HAIR)

This is a Long-Haired variety recognized in the United States but not in Europe. The general standard for Long-Hairs is applied. There are four different colors.

a) *Cameo Shell (Red Chinchilla)*
The hairs on the back, the flanks, the head and the tail are red enough to give a shimmering effect. The ground color is ivory, varying in appearance rather like the Chinchilla (it is sometimes called the Red Chinchilla). The belly chest and underside of the tail have no red. There must be no tabby marks or shading. The nose and the rims of the eyes are brick red. The eyes also are copper-colored.

b) *Shaded Cameo*
The reddish points, which are much clearer than on the Tortoiseshell Cameo, give a burnt effect, shading down to whitish cream from the flanks to the belly.

c) *Smoke Cameo*
This has the same coloring as the Smoke Long-Hair (q.v.). The coat appears to be a pure red until you separate the hairs to reveal a creamy white undercoat. No tabby stripes or patches are allowed.

d) *Cameo Tabby*
The markings are the same as for the other Tabbies on a uniform white or cream undercoat. The marks are a strong red.

13. THE MAINE COON

This is an American cat which has not been officially recognized. Experts consider it to be a pure bred Angora. In New England it is thought to have been bred from a raccoon, because the cat's front claws are often divided like the raccoon. The head is pointed with round eyes, sometimes slightly slanting. The tail has the longest hairs at the base, unlike other Long-Hairs. Their first official exhibition was held in Madison Square Garden in 1895. The Central Maine Cat Club was founded in 1953 and organizes shows every year. It is a very intelligent and clever cat.

14. THE PEKE-FACE LONG-HAIRS

This variety has been recognized in the United States but not in Europe. The head should resemble a Pekinese dog: it has very broad jawbones and a high curved forehead. The short, flat nose is level with the eyes and is hidden by the full round cheeks when seen in profile. The muzzle is decidedly wrinkled and there are wrinkles below the eyes and on either side of the nose. The eyes are very large and round. The coat is either red or red tabby.

15. THE TURKISH CAT

This is a White Long-Hair with an auburn tail, ringed with slightly darker auburn, and auburn spots on the head. Most cats dislike water very much but the Turkish cat, quite the opposite, especially when young, loves swimming, and is just as happy in fast-running water as in a still pond.

Standard

Color	The coat is chalk white with no trace of yellow. The head has auburn marking with a white blaze in the centre. The pads and interior of the ears should be shell-pink. Some ring marks may appear on the colored parts and are more distinct in kittens.
Coat	Long, soft and silky down to the roots, which are of medium length, but thick.
Head	Shaped like a short wedge. Large, well-tufted ears. Long nose.
Eyes	Round, amber-colored, luminous with pink rims.
Body	Long and sturdy, with fairly long legs, round paws, well-tufted toes. The neck and shoulders of the male are very muscular.
Scale of show points	Color: 35 — coat: 20 — head: 25 — eyes: 10 — body: 10. Total: 100.

History: The Turkish Cat really does come from Turkey. It has only recently been recognized by the Governing Council of the Cat Fancy and is beginning to appear on the show bench. Several pairs imported into England have proved that these cats reproduce true to type. There are now more than three generations of the pure breed; it is not an artificially bred cat.

Long-hair,
Smoke Blue

Himalayan Cat,
see Colourpoint,
Long-hair

THE BIRMAN

This Long-Hair has a very light cream coat with brown, chocolate or lilac points like the Siamese. An essential feature of a good Birman is the white paws, like gloves.

Standard

Color	The markings of the Birman are identical with those of the Siamese. The mask, the tail and the legs are dark chestnut brown in the Seal-Point, blue-grey, chocolate or lilac in the other groups. The fawn has a golden tinge and is almost white in the Lilac-Point. The paws are gloved with white; on the hind legs the white part comes to a point on the heel.
Body	Long, but sturdy, low on short, strong legs.
Head	Broad and round, with a strong bone structure reminiscent of the Long-Hair rather than the Siamese. The nose is short and the forehead arched.
Eyes	Slightly slanting, very expressive. A fine, dark blue.
Coat	Long and silky with a thick ruff. The coat is slightly curly under the belly.
Tail	Tufted and long, jaunty.
Scale of show points	Color: 20 — body: 20 — head: 20 — eyes: 5 — coat: 25 — tail: 10. Total: 100.

History: The sacred cat of Burma appeared for the first time in Europe in 1926. It has only recently been imported into England. There is a charming legend connected with it.

Long before the birth of the Buddha, an old priest of Kittah lived in the mountains of Indochina with his white cat called Sinh. Together they meditated before a statue with sapphire-blue eyes, Ts'un-Chian-kse, the Goddess of Transmigration. One day, as he was meditating before the statue, the old priest died. The cat at once jumped up to the sacred throne, standing on the old man's white head, and the miracle of transmigration took place: the white coat of the cat changed to gold and his yellow eyes became sapphire blue like those of the goddess. His legs, muzzle and ears turned brown, the color of the earth, and only his paws remained white because they stood on the head of his master. It refused to eat and died seven days later, carrying off the perfect soul of its master. Then the hundred cats of the temple all became the same color as Sinh. Since then, whenever one of the sacred cats dies, the soul of a priest is said to accompany him to Paradise.

CARE OF THE CAT

Ownership of a cat carries with it a number of responsibilities. They are not very arduous or complicated, but before you decide to link your life with that of a cat, it is worth stopping and considering them. You will have to feed your cat properly every day; groom him once or twice a day, depending on the breed you choose; see that he is healthy and, if you live in an apartment, clean out his toilet-tray, and, of course, allow him a reasonable amount of comfort. It is also wise, if you are one of a family, to make sure that the addition is wanted, or at the very least, accepted by everyone.

CHOICE

Your reason for wishing to possess a cat will obviously decide what kind you would like. If you want a cat for the sole purpose of catching rats and mice you should look for a strong, ordinary cat, if possible striped. If it must be a pure breed as well, choose a Siamese, because they are excellent hunters. However, if it is a companion that is wanted, choose whatever breed you fancy, even a common alley-cat.

a) *If You Have A Weakness for Alley-cats*
As soon as you let it be known that you are thinking of acquiring a cat, you will hear that a neighbor's cat just had kittens and that you can come and choose one; this is especially true if it happens to be spring or early fall.

You can also go immediately to one of the Animal Protection Societies, where you will find a heart-breaking choice of orphans waiting for an owner. But remember your responsibilities, and be careful not to bring home two or three!

b) *If You Want A Pure-Bred Cat*
In this case you must find a breeder, and the price will depend on the variety and purity of the strain.

The best ratters are European tabbies (below) or Siamese, if pedigree is essential.

203

Stray cats...

A pedigree cat will be expensive. Recent regulations now control the sale of cats to make sure the buyer gets a healthy specimen.

HOW TO CHOOSE A KITTEN

Whatever the breed, never accept a kitten under six weeks old. Wait until it is two-and-a-half to three months old when it is properly weaned. Provided the mother is properly fed, it is far better for your kitten to continue suckling until he is about three months old. You can tell the approximate age of a kitten by its teeth, all of which should have appeared by this time; both jaws should have full sets of small pointed white teeth before you bring the kitten home, in order to avoid weakness or digestive troubles later on, caused by incorrect weaning.

MALE OR FEMALE?

Females are cheaper than males. However, the inconvenience of their frequent pregnancies is no longer so great a problem as it used to be, because, although the sterilization operation is more serious than in the male, a good veterinary surgeon can do it successfully when the female is six or seven months old.

Whether cats are male or female, sterilization makes them quieter and more affectionate, and it is almost always a necessary procedure if cats are to live in an apartment.

Before you bring home your kitten, whether it comes from a cattery or a friend, make sure that it has a strong constitution and is in good health; eyes should be clear and brilliant, ears clean and odorless; the coat silky, not rough, the belly firm and elastic, neither hard nor soft.

204

There is never, alas,
any shortage of
orphans...

FIRST CONTACTS

Do not make sudden movements or noises. A basic rule in handling a cat is quietness. Allow him time to get used to his new surroundings. For him, it is an adventure into the unknown, and therefore frightening. Follow him as he explores; his curiosity is stronger than his fear, so talk quietly to him. He

It is best to wait until a kitten is two or three months old before choosing from a litter.

Allow the cat time to get accustomed to his new home and owner.

has to get to know you, your voice and your house, all at once. It is very important to talk to cats. They do not understand your words but they catch the intonation and seem to know what you mean.

Settle him in a basket with a cushion covered with soft, washable material. Do not forget that he is used to snuggling up against his mother and the other kittens, so give him a hot water bottle at first, especially if the nights are cold. Talk to him gently without holding him, and do this frequently but not for too long each time. Do not hold him in your arms if he struggles, and let him sleep as much as he wants; sleep is vital to him.

TRAINING

Animals, like humans, should start their training young.

Cats are by nature very clean. As soon as a kitten can walk, usually about four weeks old, the mother teaches him to use his tray. It should be flat, firm, solid and filled with cat-litter, sawdust, peat or sand. Cat-litter makes the least mess around the tray because it does not stick to the cats' paws. Kittens usually learn by watching their mother, who often makes onomatopoeic noises to explain what she is doing. I have seen kittens go straight to the tray without having to be shown at all.

If you have bought or adopted a kitten, it is wise to teach it yourself as soon as it arrives, because the change in surroundings will probably have upset him and it is necessary to reorganize his habits.

If you see that the cat is about to forget where he is, or has already forgotten, then carry him to his tray and make him scratch with his two front paws, explaining to him what you mean. You must try to convince him without raising your voice or being angry. Usually one lesson is enough, sometimes two, if you have a very frightened kitten. When, later on, he goes to his tray unbidden, stroke and praise him. He will realize that he is now house-trained. Be sure to disinfect the other place and treat it with deodorant. It is essential to keep your cat's tray very clean. Cats do not like dirt. Renew the litter as often as necessary and carefully wash the bowl so that it does not smell.

See that the tray is big enough so that, as the kitten grows, he has room to use it comfortably. If it gets too small he may make a mess beside it which does not mean he is dirty; he knows perfectly well where he should go to, and is trying to tell you by the only means at his disposal.

At first he will sleep in the basket, but later on he is likely to choose a place for himself: a low chair,

◀◀
You can tell the age of a kitten by its teeth. It should have a complete set of teeth before it is finally weaned.

◀
The kitten will respond to a nice warm basket.

207

an armchair, another basket, or a corner of the carpet. Allow him to choose as far as possible, but move him from places where you do not want him to go, and right from the beginning. Do not strike him, but be firm and definite, putting him down in the place he can use. Then stroke him and explain softly the reason for being moved.

Another important rule is to feed him at fixed times. If cats are in an apartment it is easy. If you live in the country, or in an area where you can allow your cat to wander off at will then he must be trained from the beginning to return regularly for meals. Should he arrive in the middle of the afternoon, give him water and explain that he will have to wait for dinner. He will soon become accustomed to the proper time.

He must also be trained to come in at night. Unless you live on a farm where the outbuildings or hayloft make a warm and scented bed for him, your cat should sleep at home. In any case it is cruel to leave a cat out at night, particularly if it is wet and cold. There are a variety of other rational reasons for bringing him in: another point is that cats attack the birds at dawn when they come down for their first feed, so if you like birds, keep your cat inside. At certain periods of the year the noise of prowling cats

After a while the cat will choose its own favourite place to sleep.

Cats do not always find closed doors insurmountable hurdles to getting out of a room.

may disturb your neighbor's, let alone your own, sleep. Finally there is the ever-present risk of the cat being run over.

The cat is an intelligent animal and soon learns what is right and wrong. Never tease him, and never hit him except for very serious reasons. Nor should you correct him if you are not sure it is his fault. In any case if punishment is to do any good it must be

Gottfried Mind:
Chat à sa Toilette.
Watercolor, 18th
century.

administered the moment the crime is committed. The animal has an innate sense of justice: he will pay only what he owes.

CARE OF THE COAT

All cats should be brushed and combed. There is no reason to neglect the daily brush just because the cat washes and cleans himself so carefully.

The cat licks himself by instinct, because it is a natural way of preventing deficiency disease, absorbing vitamin D, which accumulates on the surface of the fur, especially when the cat is exposed to the ultra-violet rays of the moon or the sun. For that reason baths and washing are not to be recommended. However, if your cat becomes dirty by accident or if he is smelly, he can certainly be washed.

Short-hairs do not seem to mind being bathed, but one should not linger over it. Avoid wetting the eyes, and wash with a special cat-shampoo or, failing this, a baby or delicate-hair shampoo, rinsing the cat carefully with warm water. Dry the cat well with a towel and afterwards with an electric hairdryer (if he will stand it), running your hand through the fur. Finally brush the hair the wrong way, and then stroke it down smoothly. Keep the cat warm for several hours afterwards to make sure both top and undercoat are absolutely dry.

If you use a dry-shampoo make sure it is specially for cats, since any other kind may block up the pores and cause mange. Afterwards brush the coat vigorously in all directions to eliminate any trace of powder.

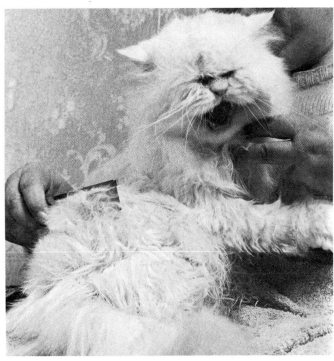

DAILY CARE

This will vary, depending on the coat.

a) *Short-hairs*
They should be brushed once a day, first the wrong way, from tail to head, to get out dead hair. Then brush the hair down with long, firm strokes, without hurting, of course. Your cat will certainly enjoy it. I know several that purr all the time.

b) *Long-hairs*
The long-haired cat needs brushing twice a day. Place the cat on a table and start by untangling firmly all the long hair with a large-toothed comb; then, using a finer comb, work through the undercoat. After combing, brush vigorously, first the wrong-

way, then from head to tail to polish the fur. Finish with a chamois for a real shine.

A long-haired cat must be brushed and combed regularly, otherwise not only its appearance, but its

Cats should be brushed once a day, at first the wrong way to get out the dead hair.

211

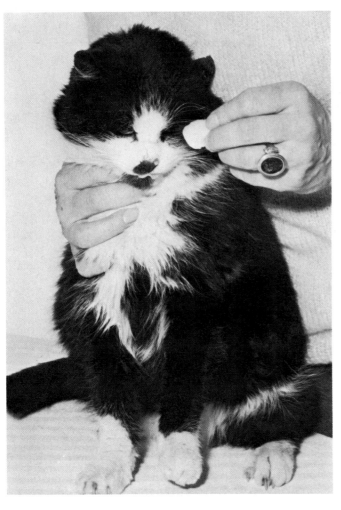

Clean the eye with a piece of cotton-wool or gauze wrung out in tepid water.

Ears can be gently cleaned of excess wax with cotton buds dipped in warm water.

Claws should also be examined. Do not cut them, but allow the cat to look after them himself since he knows exactly how far to go. Give him a wooden scratching post or piece of cork-bark. A round piece of wood, about 23 $^2/_5$ in.–29 $^3/_5$ in. high and 4 to 6 in. in diameter is attached to two boards nailed together to form a cross. Wrap a piece of old carpet round the post, with the weft on the outside, nailing it at the back. Your cat will have the pleasure of sinking his claws into a tree trunk and you can stop him from attacking your furniture and carpets.

The question of parasites is not very important for an inside cat. But as soon as your cat is free to go out anywhere, be on the watch for ticks. They can be extracted with tweezers by pinching the head which is sunk in the cat's skin. Disinfect the place afterwards. This operation is, however, very tricky and it would be advisable to get a vet to do it.

If your cat begins to scratch a great deal he probably has fleas. Insecticides can be bought at the drugstore, which will get rid of them. Afterwards the cat should be brushed vigorously. Disinfect his bed and any other places he sleeps in at the same time.

health will suffer. Both short and long-hairs require extra attention during the moult which lasts from the first season throughout the summer. At that period you can actually trim the cat by brushing the hair the wrong way for a longer period of time than during the rest of the year. You will also avoid having hairs all over the house.

Apart from its coat you should inspect your cat's ears, eyes and paws.

Eyes can be cleaned with a small piece of cotton wool or a tissue wrung out in tepid water, or tea.

Clean the ear with cotton-buds, moistened with water, taking care not to penetrate too far.

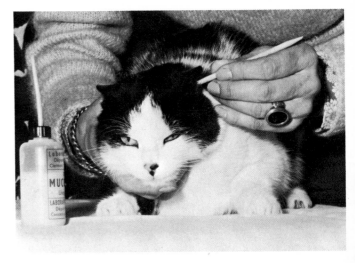

Fish is particularly good for their digestion.

FEEDING

Food plays a large part in the life of a cat. It determines the development of kittens, their resistance to disease, and the health of the adult.

In its wild state, the cat lives on a predominantly meat diet. However, its diet contains other elements, because cats eat small mammals, birds and fish whole. In addition to muscular flesh, such a diet provides blood, bone, fur and skin, offal and vegetables in a half-digested state. And like its wild relatives, the lion and the tiger, the cat starts to eat its prey by attacking the viscera, the spleen and the liver, full of blood and rich in vitamins.

Carnivores have very definite needs in their diet. They eat quantities of mineral salts, fats and nitrogenous matter which they can easily find in the wild, but which are lacking in an ordinary domestic diet. Butcher's meat alone is too monotonous and if used exclusively will cause a deficiency.

Too often we are satisfied to feed the cat—especially if there is only one—on kitchen scraps

Cats love their meat either raw or slightly warmed under the grill.

and remains of meals. A normal ration should contain all the necessary elements and be related to the weight of the animal. Cats should never be overfed, especially if they live in an apartment: 2 to 3 ounces of balanced food given twice a day should be enough for a cat of about 6 to 8 pounds. It is wise to feed at a rhythm which suits your own: noon and evening, with perhaps a little milk or yoghourt in the morning. If everyone is fed together the cat will be closer to his owners.

Raw or Cooked Food

Raw food is best. A cat in the wild does not wait to cook its birds!

If a cat is always fed cooked food, his constitution will suffer, and he may have deformed bones and teeth. Females fed only on cooked foods produce only a very few, and often rather sickly kittens which may not even survive birth.

Meat is an essential element in the diet, raw, or very lightly grilled so it is warmed through. Beef, horse, lamb, rabbit, and chicken are all acceptable. Liver and fish should be given from time to time. Lites and spleen (melt) are not recommended since their nutritional value is very limited. Raw eggs, very fresh, make a good supplement for kittens and pregnant cats.

Vegetables should be added to raw meat to round out the cat's diet, preferably green, but if dried, they should be cooked. Raw carrots can be grated in to the feed. Asparagus, endive, leeks, and cooked lettuce should all be carefully chopped and mixed with fresh mince in the ratio of about a quarter to one third of vegetable to three-quarters to two thirds of meat, depending on the taste of your cat. The amount of vegetables can be increased gradually for a cat unused to this kind of diet. Only small amounts of boiled milk and oatmeal should be given. As a general rule it is best to avoid carbohydrates.

214

Theban Tomb at
Nakht. Egyptian
cats hung their
tails in the water to
attract the fish and
then snatched them
from the water with
their claws.

Most cats love
milk, but too much
is bad for the
digestive organs.
Right: *Déjeuner du
Chat,* by Gérard.

216

Tinned Foods

Feline dietetics are making more and more progress. Many different kinds of tinned food are being manufactured in response to the cat's desire for variety. The contents are mostly fish, meat and liver, but they usually also contain vegetables and mineral salts; these latter constitute perhaps their most valuable element.

Like the human body, every function of the organs and tissues of an animal is controlled by exact molecular movement of inorganic substances. Any disturbance in the way these substances work produces an imbalance which in turn causes illness. The addition of mineral salts, which are often deficient in the normal diet, corrects this imbalance and helps keep the animal healthy. Many cats fed almost entirely on prepared cat food enjoy splendid health.

However, fresh food, provided that it is really fresh, although not indispensable, is nevertheless to be recommended. Fed alternately with tinned food, it makes a more interesting menu.

Whatever food you have chosen, or whatever your cat's taste has imposed on you, you should offer it to him barely warmed. Never give him anything hot, even if your hungry cat tries to eat it boiling. Nor should you give him iced milk straight from the refrigerator. Add some warm water to it. This dilution has the advantage of making milk easier for cats to digest, since they normally find it difficult. But do not imagine that he should have skimmed milk. He knows the difference at once; while he will drink whole milk, diluted with water, he will not touch warmed-up skimmed milk. Try it yourself, you will soon see why!

Whatever preference your cat may show for certain foods you should try to get him used to a varied diet. Like us, diversity in the diet makes for good health. If he refuses a food, often because he is not familiar with it, do not force him, but don't give up either. Offer it to him on a day when he is very hungry as a tidbit, in your fingers if you like, telling him how good it is. Cats like to be talked to. Nine times out of ten he will make an effort to taste it just to please you, and he may find that he likes it.

There should always be a pot of grass growing in an apartment for the cat. Eating a few stalks every day helps to get rid of the hairs every cat swallows in washing, and is good for his digestion.

MOVING THE CAT

MOVING HOUSE

The cat is renowned for disliking a move from his familiar surroundings. But if a cat trusts his owners and is friendly, there should be no insurmountable difficulties. It will be necessary to give him time to get accustomed to the new home, and when he has explored everywhere and rediscovered his own furniture, reassured by the sound of your voice, he will settle down and begin to wash. Then you can give him something to eat in his new kitchen, but use his own plate. As soon as he begins to eat you can breathe a sigh of relief; your cat has accepted his

Siamese cats feeding. Ideally every animal has its own bowl.

new home. Nevertheless it is wise not to let him out for several days, until you are sure that he will not run away.

If your cat does escape, despite all your precautions, get in touch with your old neighbors. It is known for cats to travel immense distances to get back to their old home. It is a good idea, during the period of adaptation, to make him wear an elastic collar with your name, address and telephone number.

HOLIDAYS

Do not forget your cat when you go on holiday. Just leaving him with enough food, shut up in your apartment or in another safe place, is no solution. The cat will eat up the whole lot at once and then go hungry. Friends or neighbors can come and feed him but they must stay and keep him company for a while. Cats hate being alone and become terribly bored. The best solution is for someone the cat knows to come and live in your house with the cat. Otherwise you can board him in a good cattery.

MEANS OF TRANSPORT

The Car: You must train the cat to travel in the car from an early age. Begin by allowing him to get in when the car is stationary and the engine turned off. Let him get used to the car as an extension of his own home, a room like the rest. Later start the engine. If the cat is not too nervous, move forward a little, then stop. Do not force the cat, of course, but keep trying. Gradually you will be able to make short journeys. In the end when the cat is quite adjusted and at ease in the car you will be able to undertake long journeys without any trouble. He will develop the habit of lying on the shelf at the

back or on a cushion placed for him on the back seat, or even on the knees of your passenger. If you are quite alone it is wiser, except in very special cases, to put him in a basket in case he should get in the way while you are driving.

Do not give him a large meal before leaving; it is preferable for him to have half the usual amount. If your cat vomits when travelling ask your vet or druggist for an anti-sickness tablet to give him before leaving. For long journeys you can also add a tranquillizer.

Aeroplane: No animals are allowed to travel with the passengers. They are all placed in comfortable cages in the storage area. If possible, give your cat something familiar to comfort him while he is alone.

Boat: Here there is no difficulty. You can keep the cat in your cabin.

Train: Cats travel free on the train and in buses. However, they should be in a basket.

FORMALITIES FOR TRAVEL ABROAD

At the border of each country you will have to show a veterinary certificate of health. Some countries also

Cats dislike moving houses, but when they start to wash, this proves the new home is accepted.

A harness is
preferable to a
collar if you want
to put the cat on a
lead.

demand an anti-rabies certificate for all cats over six months. This vaccination is given twice, with a fortnight between each, and the second injection must take place at least a month before the date of entry. It is a precaution to be taken about two months before your departure.

CONTAINERS

If the journey is only a short one you can put your cat in a carrying case with a zipper, allowing enough room for him to put his head out. If he can see what is going on round him, he won't be so frightened, but you must watch him to see that he does not escape.

For long journeys you will need a travelling case, which can be bought in pet-shops. Choose one large

enough for the cat to move around in and cover the bottom with a cushion or folded blanket. In winter you may also cover the sides and back, in order to protect him from draughts—though do leave the 'window' open.

During the journey, open the basket from time to time, stroke and talk to the cat. The touch of your hand and the sound of your voice will help him to endure the trip patiently.

Some cats, especially Siamese, can be easily trained to use a harness and lead. You ought to prepare for this as soon as you have the kitten, because they must

An overnight bag is adequate for short journeys, but long ones necessitate a special basket.

223

The mother carries her kittens by the neck.

learn while young; it is extremely difficult to get an adult cat to tolerate any harness. I would recommend a harness rather than a collar, because the training is easier: cats find it more difficult to get out of harness than a collar and if they pull on the lead, they won't strangle themselves. This is the best solution to travel problems, and makes moving a cat no more difficult than moving a dog.

NUTRITION, HEALTH AND ILLNESS

It is not sufficient just to give a cat enough to eat and a place to sleep. You must study your cat's behavior and pay attention to changes in his appearance. The cat is not an animal that complains much; but if your cat is miserable and depressed with dull eye and staring coat, and if he is not behaving normally within twenty-four hours, he is most probably ill.

However, unless he is obviously in pain do not worry too much if your cat refuses food for twenty-four hours. It may only be indigestion, and in that case he will be back on his feet again, at the worst, by the next day. However, should the condition persist, take his temperature and if it is above 102.2 °F (39 °C), call your vet.

Disease does not usually appear without warning. There is a period of incubation, during which the whole organism is gradually invaded by the ailment and, after that, the illness becomes apparent and can be diagnosed. It is usually between these two periods that you will first notice symptoms. Then you must watch the animal, try to assess how serious his condition is and decide whether to go to the vet. Immediate attention is the surest means to a cure. Far too many cats, that could have been saved, die from sheer negligence.

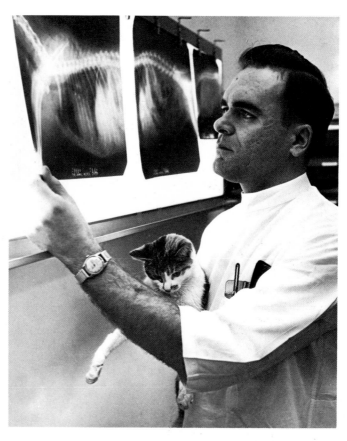

The cat is not a complaining animal, so if he looks morose and his coat is dull, waste no time in taking him to the vet.

THE PRINCIPAL SYMPTOMS OF SICKNESS

a) *Loss of Appetite:* If the loss of appetite lasts longer than one day, take the cat's temperature (normal 100.4° to 101.8 °F or 38° to 38.8 °C), inspect the inside of his mouth, and examine the urine and faeces.

b) *General Depression:* If it persists and gets worse after twenty-four hours take the animal to the vet at once.

c) *Staring and Moulting Coat:* Review the diet, see that the cat is not constipated, and ask the vet for vitamins.

d) *Diarrhoea:* Give yeast and yoghourt and, if the cat is young, look for worms. If the condition persists, with a high temperature and evil-smelling faeces showing traces of blood, consult the vet at once. It could be serious blood-poisoning or enteritis.

e) *Vomiting:* After meals, this may be due to indigestion: the rejected food is undigested and mixed with mucus and froth. At other times, if the rejected material is yellowish, liquid or frothy, it may be a sign of a liver disorder or typhus. If the material is brownish and smells strong, it may be caused by intestinal occlusion, or uraemia. Call the vet without delay.

f) *Intense thirst:* This is a serious symptom indicating chronic nephritis, gastritis, uraemia or fever.

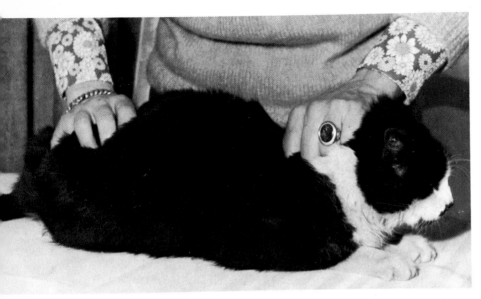

Holding the cat for
examination or
administering
medicine.

g) *Sneezing:* If the eyes water and the nose runs, the condition is coryza.

h) *Coughing:* Whether the cough is dry or soft, take the cat's temperature. If the cough continues after a dose of cough-medicine, consult the vet.

i) *Panting:* If the condition persists, and especially if the animal is old, ask the vet to examine its heart and chest.

j) *Scratching:* If the animal scratches all over, it may have eczema. If it confines its attention to the neck and head, it is probably only mange.

k) *Scratching of the ears:* Inspect the ears. If there is a brown deposit inside it is auricular mange; if the deposit is yellow and evil-smelling it is otitis.

l) *Urine:* If the cat finds it painful to pass water and there is blood in the urine, he may have cystitis or stone. Very dark, strong-smelling urine in small quantities denotes kidney disease. Feel the back behind the ribs gently to find out whether the area of the kidneys is painful.

Very abundant, pale urine, accompanied by thirst and wastage, denotes a chronic nephritis, especially in the case of an old cat. Diabetes is rare in cats.

PRACTICAL ADVICE

HOW TO LOOK AFTER A CAT

The cat is not an easy animal to examine. Even the most gentle and loving cat gets very upset if you try to subject him to any kind of serious examination, administer medicine or apply a dressing.

As far as possible you must try to be cunning, patient and quick. If that does not work, he must be controlled in a kind, but firmer manner. The best way to keep a cat still is to hold the skin behind the ears in the hand and hold him firmly on the table by pressing gently on his back. You will need to be firm, so that the cat realizes he is dealing with someone stronger than himself and that it is useless to struggle.

To examine the mouth and ears, one person must stand behind the animal, take a front paw in each hand and hold the legs and elbows back towards the animal's body. In extreme cases the cat can be put into a special bag.

TAKING THE TEMPERATURE

Temperature is taken in the rectum using an ordinary clinical thermometer smeared with a little vaseline. It is best to get someone else to hold the animal. Then lift the cat's tail, introduce the thermometer a quarter of its length and hold it there for a minute.

The temperature should be taken at a fixed time, preferably before feeding in the morning, before the animal has had time to get tired. In the evening let it sleep for an hour before taking the temperature.

Taking the temperature.

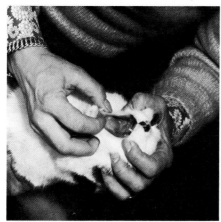

Examining the mouth.

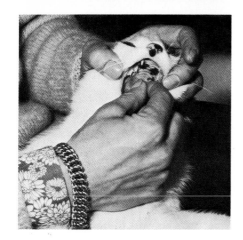

Giving a pill.

ADMINISTERING MEDICINE

a) *Pills and Tablets:* You can always try to conceal them in a piece of meat, but usually the cat will eat the meat and spit out the pill. In that case he must be made to take it.

Take the cat's head in the left hand, pull it gently backwards introducing the thumb and middle finger on either side of the jaw to hold the mouth open. Holding the pill between thumb and forefinger of the right hand, press on the lower jaw with your middle finger and put the pill far back on the tongue, if possible at the point where swallowing is automatic. Then shut the mouth and hold it closed until the pill has been swallowed. When it has gone, give a mouthful of milk.

b) *Liquids:* First try to mix them with the food or drink. Some cats will take them like that. Others have to be forced.

Hold the cat firmly and introduce the liquid through the open lips with a syringe or ear-dropper. If you are alone, wrap the animal in a strong towel and hold it between your legs. This is also a good way of administering pills.

c) *Suppositories:* It is necessary for someone else to hold the cat while you lift the tail and introduce the suppository, smeared with vaseline, as deeply as possible into the anus. Then put the tail down between the back legs pressing it against the anus to prevent its expulsion.

d) *Injections:* 1. *Sub-cutaneous:* Injections are given either in the flanks or at the back of the neck. It will be necessary for someone to hold the animal firmly.

Prepare the syringe, then disinfect the area by swabbing around under the fur with surgical spirit. (It is best to pour it on, since cotton wool sometimes fails to penetrate the fur.) Take a fold of skin between the thumb and index finger of your left hand and insert the needle cleanly, keeping the angle of the syringe parallel to the skin. Inject slowly. As it

227

penetrates, the liquid will form a bubble below the skin. It is best not to touch it, but to leave it to be absorbed.

2. *Intra-muscular:* The best place is the lumbar region, halfway between the top of the spine and the end of the lumbar muscle. Inject downwards to the animal. If you are not experienced, take the animal to the vet.

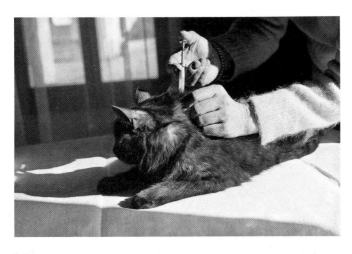

Sub-cutaneous injection.

3. *Intra-venous:* Only a vet is in a position to carry out this operation.

e) *Dressings:* Cats dislike dressings. The difficulty is that a loose dressing will not hold, but, on the other hand, if it is too tight it will not only be a source of annoyance, but may cause gangrene. So generally bandages are to be avoided. It is preferable to use plaster applied direct to the skin, spreading out the gauze over the wound. Always use gauze on a wound, never cotton wool, and especially not wool or nylon cloth.

Dressings following serious operations will either be done by your vet or he will tell you how to do it.

GENERAL ILLNESSES

FELINE ENTERITIS

This disease, often epidemic, is caused by a virus. It is very serious, very contagious, and quickly fatal. Only a vet can save the animal, and then only if he can make early diagnosis.

Symptoms: The cat is depressed, does not eat, and hides in a dark corner. The coat is dull and the temperature rises as high at 105.8 °F (41 °C). In the terminal stages it can fall to 98.6 °F (37 °C). Vomit is foamy, full of bile, and the diarrhoea evil-smelling. The animal suffers from acute thirst, but cannot drink without vomiting. It dehydrates very quickly.

Treatment: Call the vet immediately. While waiting, wrap your cat in a woollen blanket and keep him warm with hot water bottles. The vet will give antibiotics, heart stimulants and try to rehydrate the animal.

Prevention: Have your cat vaccinated after it is two months old and at regular intervals; ask the vet to send you a reminder when it is necessary. The vaccines are extremely good and there is no risk. It is the only way to avoid infection, whatever the breed of cat.

Keep the food tray clean and do not let it lie about after he has eaten. It will be infected by dust and flies which carry the disease.

TUBERCULOSIS

This is a contagious disease contracted by eating dirty refuse or contaminated meat or milk. Tuberculosis can be transmitted from man to cat and vice versa.

Symptoms: The animal wastes away, while still eating. It has a dry and intermittent cough, chronic diarrhoea and sores on the face and neck that will not heal. The temperature is slightly above normal: 101.8 °F to 102.6 °F (38.8 °C to 39.2 °C).

Treatment: The vet will make a test. If it is positive it is necessary to isolate the animal away from the house and treat it with recognized antitubercular medicines.

URAEMIA

This is usually found in old cats whose kidneys are no longer functioning properly.

Symptoms: Frequent vomiting, intense thirst, mouth ulcers, bad breath, sub-normal temperature, wasting, urine very pale, passed in frequent but small quantities, or complete anuresis and nervous trouble.

Treatment: Make a blood test to find out the concentration of urea which may often be above a few drops per quart. In an old cat it is often the sign of approaching death. Treatment may relieve his discomfort, but will not cure him. In the case of a young cat it is necessary to discover the reason for renal failure and to treat him for excess urea by giving him diuretics.

RABIES

This is a viral disease, very contagious, which is transmitted by biting, because the virus cannot penetrate either a healthy skin or membrane.

The incubation period is very variable.

Symptoms: Restlessness, attempts to escape, aggressive tendencies. Saliva runs abundantly, refusal to drink, accompanied by a strange cry. Paralysis and death.

Treatment: None known. Vaccination is the sole method of preventing this disease and is obligatory if crossing frontiers. A number of countries will not allow an animal to enter, or to return, unless it has been vaccinated.

The vaccine is administered in two doses at fortnightly intervals. At the time of entry the certificate has to be dated more than a month before and less than six months. Re-vaccination is annual and needs only one injection.

TUMORS

They are often found on the teats and are of several kinds.

a) *Benign Tumors:* They grow slowly cause no discomfort and have no tendency to spread.

Treatment: Surgery is the only effective treatment and can be carried out without danger.

b) *Malignant Tumors:* These grow around a principal tumor and are usually carcinogenic.

Wounded cat with a dressing.

Treatment: If taken in time surgery is often successful. Depending on their type one can usually cure tumors on the breasts, testicles or ovaries, spleen, intestines and genital organs, but liver and chest tumors are almost always fatal.

POISONING

A cat can be poisoned by eating poisoned rodents or grass in fields that have been treated with pesticides, it may eat strychnine intended for rodents and foxes, or eat rats already poisoned with warfarin.

a) *Strychnine Poisoning:* Death is almost instantaneous and the animal must be treated within a quarter of an hour. The poison causes convulsions in which the legs stiffen spasmodically, and the spinal column twists into an arc.

Treatment: Stomach pump and application of antidotes.

b) *Arsenical Poisoning:* Excess salivating, overall weakness, colic and paralysis.

Treatment: Administer every quarter of an hour a spoonful of albumen water made by mixing beaten egg whites into a glass of water.

c) *Phosphoric Poisoning:* The cat is intensely thirsty, the membranes of the mouth are swollen and vomiting occurs. This is followed by severe trembling and collapse of the hind-quarters.

Treatment: Consult your vet.

SKIN DISEASES

These can be divided into parasitic and non-parasitic.

Non-Parasitic
Eczema: This is a very common complaint, the cause of which is not always easy to diagnose because its symptoms vary. Generally it is caused by bad feeding. It is recognized by an acute or chronic inflammation of the skin.

a) *Acute Eczema:* This is usually found in young cats and starts with small red patches, covered with suppurating blisters. The pus smells bad, mats the fur and makes yellow scabs.

b) *Chronic Eczema:* This only occurs with old cats. Sometimes it follows acute eczema, but generally appears directly. It starts with the hair coming out on the back, and the rest of the coat becoming broken, dull and falling.

c) *Eczema of the Ear:* see *Aural catarrh* (p. 240)

The first thing is to adjust the diet. Eliminate all carbohydrate: pastry, potatoes (which should be never be given to cats), bread, cake. Cut the amount of food by half, administer yoghourt mixed with a little meat and raw fish. Apply a solution of alum at the rate of 1 scant tablespoon per quart, or iodized glycerine on the wounds and sores, then a hydrocortisone or penicillin-based powder or liquid. Do not use greasy ointment, which prevents the skin from breathing and the wounds from drying out.

WOUNDS AND SORES:

see *Injury to the Locomotive System* (p. 240)

PARASITIC DISEASES

A well-cared-for cat will rarely catch fleas and lice even less frequently. However, among animals living alone and abandoned in big cities, fleas proliferate. Fleas are a great inconvenience for the animal and man, because they jump from one to the other. They are bad for the cat because they make it irritable and carry disease.

Symptoms: If your cat scratches a lot and rather violently in a particular place, then turns its head quickly to lick, there is a good chance that the cause is fleas.

Treatment: There are numerous effective insecticidal powders on sale in drugstores. To make sure that the treatment works, wrap the cat in a towel after applying the powder, leaving only the head protruding. Afterwards rub him all over with a damp sponge, so that he does not lick the insecticide which is always more or less toxic to cats. When he is dry, comb with a very fine comb to get rid of dead fleas. The best way of killing fleas is to bathe the cat, using a good shampoo to which you have added a flea-killer.

You must also disinfect all the bedding and any place where your cat is accustomed to sleep at the same time.

Ticks: These parasites attach themselves to cats when they go into the fields. Ticks live on blood which they suck by hooking themselves into the skin. They carry disease which they transmit as they pierce the skin. They must be treated at once.

Treatment: In order to kill a tick cover it with a drop of insecticide, petrol, or fine salt. It collapses of

its own accord after a few seconds. You can then get rid of it by using tweezers, but be careful to remove the head by holding it close to the skin. If the animal is badly infested an anti-parasite bath will be necessary.

MANGE (Caused by *notoedres cati,* a mite)

Mange generally appears on the nape of the neck, the ears, forehead and face but rarely goes below the neck.

Symptoms: It is recognized by falling hair with grey suppurating scabs. The skin quickly becomes hard, thick and wrinkled. The cat scratches furiously, tearing all the sores, and becomes very distressed. It is depressed, refuses food and will ultimately die of attrition if the disease is not quickly controlled.

Treatment: Wash off as many scabs as possible with tepid water, dry the skin and apply an ointment prescribed by the vet. Nowadays a lindane-based ointment is replacing those based on juniper-oil, sulphur and Peruvian balm.

RINGWORM

Ringworm is not so common as mange but is very contagious and can be transmitted from man to cats. The patches are few and not large as in mange. There are three different kinds but the commonest is the scab type which usually starts on the belly and on the paws.

Symptoms: Recognizable by bald patches, where the skin is delicate, often red with greyish scabs. Patches appear in several parts of the body.

Treatment: If you catch it early, ringworm can be treated with applications of tincture of iodine. If this is not effective you should ask the vet for oral antibiotics.

If a cat scratches he may only have fleas but it could be mange.

Feline influenza is very dangerous and cats should be vaccinated against it.

RESPIRATORY DISEASES

As a general rule all respiratory disorders in the cat are serious and should be treated immediately by the vet. Never allow your cat to cough over a long period without taking advice.

CORYZA *(Feline Influenza)*

Coryza is an inflammation of the nasal cavities which can be recognized by incessant sneezing and running nose, at first serous, then mucous and in the end purulent. Sometimes it is a benign infection, in which case the cat's general condition remains fairly good, and the cat will recover completely if kept in a warm, humid atmosphere for a few days and given inhalants. Avoid the application of menthol cream or any vaseline to the nostrils.

However, it is more likely to be feline influenza which is highly contagious.

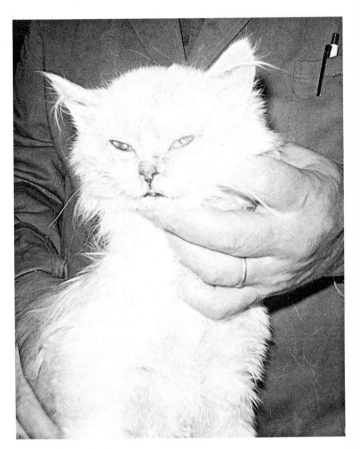

A cat with mange will die of exhaustion if not properly treated.

Symptoms: It starts in the same way as ordinary coryza, but after a day or two the animal loses his appetite, the temperature rises to 104 °F (40 °C) the nose is completely blocked and the cat can only breathe through the mouth. The throat is sore and the eyes discharge; the animal refuses all food, breathes with increasing difficulty, coughs and is completely prostrated.

Treatment: It is advisable to refrain from taking the cat to the surgery, but to call in the vet and avoid passing on the infection. The vet will administer suitable antibiotics and provide tonics and vitamins to improve the general condition.

Avoid Infection: Keep the cat in isolation. Wash your hands and change your clothes if you have to handle

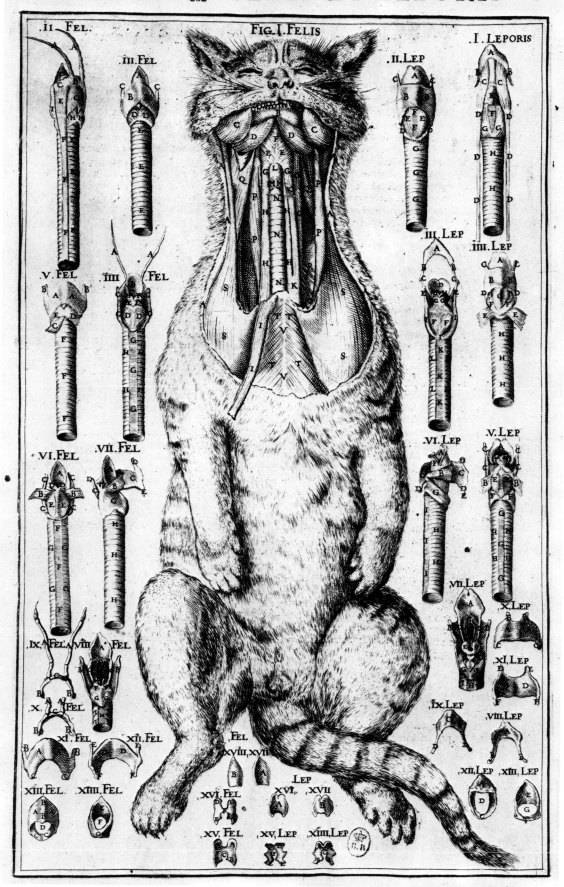

Anatomical drawing from *L'Histoire générale de la Médecine,* showing the cats respiratory system.

233

other animals. Have your cats vaccinated against feline influenza. Some catteries will not accept boarders unless they have a vaccination certificate.

TONSILITIS

Symptoms: The cat has a dry and repeated cough which causes vomiting of mucus. It has difficulty swallowing, with a sore throat and slight temperature.
Treatment: If the cough persists it will be necessary to consult the vet.

BRONCHITIS

Bronchitis usually makes its appearance in spring and fall when temperatures rise and fall suddenly. It is caused by a lowering of the body temperature when the weather is cold and wet.
Symptoms: It starts with general discomfort, shivering, a dry cough turning to a moist cough, breathlessness and a rise in temperature, not very high, but constant, to between 102.2 °F and 104 °F (39 °-40 °C).
Treatment: Keep the animal warm and out of the damp or sudden changes of temperature. The vet will administer antibiotics and decongestants. While waiting for the vet, give some children's cough mixture.

In old cats repeated doses of bronchitis occur if the animal is not treated quickly. It then becomes chronic, in association with tuberculosis. If bronchitis is neglected it may degenerate into bronchial-pneumonia, a serious condition which will be fatal if not treated quickly and efficiently. Call the vet at once. Bronchial-pneumonia can also develop independently. It may also follow feline influenza.

DISEASES OF THE DIGESTIVE SYSTEM

Foreign bodies: These are usually fish-bones or pieces of bone that get lodged between the teeth or in the palate.
Symptoms: The animal makes desperate attempts to dislodge the bone with its front paws. He will try to vomit, salivating violently.
Treatment: Open the animal's mouth and see which way the bone is lying, then extract it gently. Disinfect the wound. The foreign body may also be a lump, not sharp, but large enough to block the oesophagus, stomach or intestine. In that case treatment is much more difficult and only a vet will know the correct procedure, which may well require surgery.

GASTRO-ENTERITIS

Young cats are particularly susceptible. This condition is often provoked by eating indigestible or rotten food, and also by cold. Sometimes it is caused by a microbe and then it is difficult to distinguish it from feline enteritis, since the symptoms are similar.
Symptoms: The cat is very depressed; it refuses all food and suffers from violent thirst. The breath smells bad and the temperature may be as high as 104 °F to 105.8 °F (40 ° to 41 °C). The subjects vomits frequently, has diarrhoea, and the stomach is tender to the touch. The cat is restless, seeking a cool place to lie.
Treatment: Professional treatment is essential to relieve the serious effects of dehydration provoked by sickness and diarrhoea. Also the cat must have antibiotics. After the crisis has passed, see to the animal's diet, eliminating farinaceous food (bread, pastry, potatoes), an excess of which often causes this disease. Give him raw meat, slightly heated in a grill pan with no oil, meat broth and vegetables, as well

as vitamins B and C, to encourage the always rather slow convalescence.

CONSTIPATION

Older cats frequently get constipated, as do cats living in apartments where they live a very sedentary life and take almost no exercise. It can also be caused by hair-balls, which can be avoided by careful brushing and combing, especially in Long-Hairs and during the moult.

Symptoms: Bowel movements are hard, difficult and incomplete. It produces an accumulation of waste in the large intestine making the belly swollen and painful. In the most serious cases the animal refuses food, vomiting frequently. That is occlusion and causes death by auto-intoxication.

Treatment: If it is treated at once constipation is rarely fatal and liquid paraffin is usually effective. Rehydration of the intestinal tract can be tried, also enemas, but they are very difficult to manage with a cat. Suppository laxatives are easier to handle. In very serious cases the vet may have to operate to free the blockage. It is a very delicate operation.

LIVER DISEASES

The liver is important, its role as an antitoxic agent and sugar-transformer means that the organism depends absolutely on its functioning properly.

Hepatitis (Inflammation of the liver): This may be caused by eating insecticides or unsuitable medicine, or it may be infectious and produce jaundice.

Symptoms: Jaundice can be recognized by a yellowing of the skin and membranes. It is caused by anything that obstructs the flow of bile, which is retained in the liver and partially absorbed by the blood. Vomiting, depression and fever follow.

Treatment: Only a qualified vet can diagnose and treat this illness.

INTESTINAL PARASITES

The stomach and intestine of the cat harbor parasites which produce diarrhoea, colic, nervous attacks, intestinal perforation and growing troubles.

Most of these parasites are worms, either flat or round. Examination of the faeces will generally decide which, and it is essential to know since the treatment will vary.

ROUNDWORMS

The cat is infested directly by absorbing eggs or embryonic worms living in water or food or brought home by a carrier.

Ascaris Mystax is the most common roundworm. It measures $1\,^3/_5$ to $3\,^9/_{10}$ inches long and infests the small intestine, especially in young cats. As soon as the eggs reach the intestine they turn into larvae. Then they follow a cycle passing through several organs, one being the liver, and more particularly through the lungs and into the bronchial tubes where they are vomited from the trachaea. If the infestation is slight no great harm is done. However if it is bad the cat shows clinical symptoms.

Symptoms: Bronchial cough as the larvae pass into the respiratory organs, diarrhoea, vomiting, and nervous attacks as soon as the adult worm passes into the intestine. It should be noted that absence of worms in the faeces does not mean that the animal is not infested, because they may have been passed in the shape of eggs invisible to the naked eye, or they may still be in the larval stage.

If the *ascaris* become too numerous they can cause obstruction in the intestine. Unlike *Ascaris, Ankylo-*

stomes (hook-worm) is from $^2/_5$ to $^4/_5$ inches long, and remains fixed to the intestinal wall. It is very difficult to detect, and the eggs can only be seen by examination of the faeces. They live on blood and can cause pernicious anaemia. They are, fortunately, rare in Europe and the United States.

TAPE WORM OR TAENIA

The larva passes through an intermediate host of a different species before the adult infests the cat. Cats become infested by eating viscera of herbivores or rodents, or by swallowing fleas. There are several kinds of *Taenia*, of which the following are the principal varieties:
Taenia crassicollis: The larva feeds on the liver of small rodents.
Taenia Echinococcus: This measures only a fraction of an inch. Its larva lives in the liver of ruminants and of man.
Taenia Bothriocephalus: A rare species, the larva inhabiting fish liver.
Symptoms: A tapeworm can easily be detected in the cat by examining the faeces. Flat white rings, looking like noodles or rice stand out clearly on the top of the faeces. They can also sometimes be seen sticking to the region of the anus. You should see that your cat does not waste away, have a capricious appetite or suffer from attacks of diarrhoea. Occasionally the animal may have convulsions.
Treatment: Excellent treatments are available in the form of tablets or drops, generally with an anti-spasmodic added to the vermifuge, to prevent the vomiting associated with worming. Sometimes the treatment has to be continued for two consecutive days. Follow the instructions of the vet, or the packet. The parasitic cycle of *Ascaria* lasts a month; it is therefore wise to repeat the treatment a month later. It should be done twice a year. Destroy the faeces of an infested animal, specially after worming, to prevent re-infestation or contamination of another animal. Do not worm a sick cat.

DISEASES OF THE KIDNEYS AND BLADDER

KIDNEYS

Diseases of the kidneys, from a simple congestion to a tumor, are always very serious and should never be neglected. Because the kidney acts as a filter for the blood, the slightest disturbance in its function can produce serious troubles which may prove fatal.

a) *Acute Nephritis*
Acute nephritis is an inflammation of the kidney often caused by a general infection or poisoning.
Symptoms: High fever and intense depression. The animal is in great pain and will not move. The urine is thick, dark and sometimes red, indicating the presence of blood which is very serious indeed. The cat refuses all food and frequently dies from uraemia.
Treatment: It is essential to seek professional advice. While waiting for the vet keep the animal warm, and apply warm cloths across the kidneys to try to alleviate the pain. Give a diuretic drink. Put the cat on a low-protein diet, increase carbohydrates. Both treatment and convalescence will be prolonged.

b) *Chronic Nephritis*
This may be the consequence of an acute nephritis, but it usually occurs from bad feeding over a number of years. It is nearly always a disease of aged cats.
Symptoms: The symptoms are less spectacular than those of acute nephritis. Urination is frequent, in

small quantities. Analysis reveals albumen, the coat is staring, the skin dry with occasional eczema. Frequent vomiting and persistent diarrhoea cause the animal to become exhausted and too feeble to move.

Treatment: This is a case for the vet who will administer antiseptics to help cleanse the kidneys and general tonics to stimulate the heart. The animal should have a milk diet with very little meat. Complete cure is fairly rare.

DISEASES OF THE BLADDER

These are less serious than diseases of the kidneys but should never be neglected.

a) *Cystitis*
This is an inflammation of the bladder produced by an infection caused either by poison or stones.
Symptoms: The cat is feverish, he passes water only with difficulty and in pain. He remains lying down. The urine is thick, smells bad, and contains both albumen and pus.
Treatment: The pain can be relieved by warm compresses applied to the belly, while waiting. The vet will administer antibiotics and general antiseptics. Keep the cat on a milk diet for the first few days, then gradually add a little raw meat. Eliminate all starchy or acid foods.

Paralysis of the Bladder
This is a disease of aged cats, especially neutered males.
Symptoms: The belly is swollen, the bladder hard and painful to the touch. The cat cannot pass water at all.
Treatment: Gently massage the bladder, pressing very lightly to evacuate the urine. The vet will carry out a probe and prescribe a tonic for the nerves.

DISEASES OF THE GENITAL ORGANS

Now that castration and spaying are more frequent many genital troubles are being avoided. However there are always some cats that have not been altered. The following notes on common illnesses may therefore be relevant.

Metritis: This is an inflammation of the uterus which may be serious whether it is acute or chronic. It usually occurs after a difficult birth or an abortion; it may be caused by a retained placenta or incomplete delivery.
Symptoms: A thick discharge of pus and blood from the vagina. This discharge is worse in chronic than acute metritis. The cat refuses food and becomes exhausted through vomiting and diarrhoea.
Treatment: The disease must be treated immediately and if it is not effective, a hysterectomy is necessary. It should be done, if possible, on a cat in good physical condition because it is a serious operation and the

Cat having kittens. The kittens are generally born at intervals of twenty to thirty minutes.

shock is great. Convalescence will be long, but afterwards the cat will be better than ever.

DIFFICULT BIRTHS

It is wise to be present when your cat has her kittens. Kittens are generally born at intervals of fifteen to twenty minutes and the number varies from one to seven or eight. The birth lasts from two to five hours.

If there is a noticeable pause in the births and the cat is having violent contractions without result, call the vet at once, because the animal will soon become exhausted. If the use of forceps fails, then a caesarian operation must be done at once. Unfortunately this makes the cat very weak and affects her lactation. The kittens will have to be fed with a bottle, using milk specially prepared for kittens.

A caesarian operation does not prevent a further pregnancy. But the cat should be allowed, or sometimes forced, to rest for some while before she is fit for a further mating.

Gestation varies from sixty-two to sixty-four days. The pregnant cat should be fed a diet rich in meat, eggs and fish with the addition of vitamins A and D in liquid form. But do not overfeed or the cat will get too fat, which is dangerous.

In the week before the kittens are due see that the cat has regular bowel movements. Should it be constipated, show loss of appetite or excessive thirst, see the vet.

In the last forty-eight hours before labour begins her temperature will fall suddenly by a degree. This is quite normal. If your cat's temperature is below 102.2° F (37.9° C), the onset of labour is close. An hour after the birth the mother should be offered a nourishing meal in her bed, because she will refuse to leave the kittens. If she will not eat, call the vet.

DISEASES OF THE NERVOUS SYSTEM

PARALYSIS

The cause of paralysis can be anything which disturbs the function of the nervous system.
Symptoms: The animal loses consciousness and movement in part of the body. Depending on the area affected he will drag his hind-quarters, or his lower jaw may hang open.
Treatment: The vet will administer the correct treatment from the appearance of the first symptoms and, provided the nervous system is not destroyed, recovery should be fairly rapid. Otherwise it is likely to be slow.

MENINGITIS

Meningitis follows an infection: feline enteritis, neglected coryza or sometimes a trauma.
Symptoms: The animal cries, dribbles and suffers from convulsions, jerking spasmodically. The appearance of the eyes is distraught, the gait tottering. This is followed by a period of depression before the cycle begins again.
Treatment: Only the vet can diagnose and treat the animal which should be kept in a dark airy room in absolute quiet.

EPILEPSY

This is generally a chronic inherited illness or it may follow an infection. It is not always fatal if the cat is young and in good condition.
Symptoms: The cat is suddenly attacked by fits of trembling, the eyes are haggard. He falls suddenly and stiffly, losing consciousness. He will remain

prostrate, in convulsions, dribbling abundantly, the neck held stiffly back. The fit generally only lasts a few minutes and the cat will get up and, after remaining dazed for a few moments, carry on as usual.

Treatment: An incurable disease, but treatment prescribed by a vet can reduce or even stop the attacks. The cat must be given anti-epilepsy pills. The treatment should never be suddenly interrupted since it will cause a recurrence of symptoms.

ECLAMPSIS

This happens just before or after a pregnant cat is in labor. The cause is not known. Symptoms resemble epilepsy, but the convulsions last longer with periods of depression. The vet will administer calcium, phosphorus and tranquillizers.

Haggard eyes are a symptom of epilepsy. Drawing by Claude Estang.

DISEASES OF THE EYE

EYELIDS

a) *Blepharitis:* The eyelids are inflamed either by a wound, eczema or following conjunctivitis. They also get sties.

Symptoms: The eyelids are swollen and weeping. In the case of a sty, the swelling, filled with pus, can easily be seen on the eyelid.

Treatment: Wash the eye with tepid, boiled water. Keep changing the cotton wool. Apply an antiseptic ointment.

b) *Conjunctivitis:* This is an inflammation of the eyelids and may be caused by a foreign body, inversion of the eyelid or a wound. It can also be caused by coryza or viral disease.

Symptoms: The eyelids are inflamed, the edges stuck down with pus, the conjunctive red and the eyes almost closed.

Treatment: First look for the cause and, if it is a foreign body, remove it. Then wash the eye with tepid, boiled water or camomile. Then drop into the eye, with a dropper, a calming antiseptic lotion or ophthalmic penicillin ointment.

c) *Extension of the third eyelid:* When this happens the eye is gradually covered by the third eyelid (called the *haw*), which is a membrane covering the eye at a perpendicular angle to the other two eyelids, starting from the inside corner of the eye.

This happens fairly frequently in the cat and usually indicates an infection, or poor condition at least. Consult the vet without delay.

OPHTHALMIA

This is usually an infection of the eye which attacks kittens at birth and which is often not detected until the kittens open their eyes. They are normally infected by the mother. It should be treated straight away lest the kitten become blind in one or both eyes.

Symptoms: The eye is stuck fast and swollen. You can see the pus if you draw aside the lids.

Treatment: Clean the eyes several times a day with boiled, tepid water, and apply eye-lotion or antibiotic ointment.

CATARACT

Cataract is an opacification of the lens which is found in cats about ten years old.

Symptoms: The eye changes color. The centre grows more bluish and the animal's vision diminishes. Cataract can lead to blindness.

Treatment: Treatment with placental extract sometimes gives good results. However, surgery is very often successful.

DISEASES OF THE EAR

Inflammation of the ear-canal, *otitis,* is generally caused by mites or eczema. Never neglect the slightest inflammation of the ear. When you wash your cat, be sure that you clean out all soapy water from the ear canal.

Otodectic mange: This is strictly local in the ear-canal, hence its name.

Symptoms: The cat shakes its head, holds it to one side, always the same. It scratches the ear with its back paw. The inside of the ear will show a dark brown exudate with an unpleasant smell. Sometimes the cat also has nervous attacks.

Treatment: Clean out the ear with tepid water and administer several drops of antiparasitic oil. Do this morning and evening, making sure that the liquid goes right into the ear. Do not give up too soon, and watch for a recurrence.

AURAL CATARRH

This is an illness connected with eczema and is usually difficult to cure.

Symptoms: The cat often holds its head to the side which is infected. Slight pressure at the base of the ear will cause considerable pain. There is a continuous brown discharge from the ear canal, which irritates the skin.

Treatment: Dry out the ear-canal every day with cotton buds, either dry or with 10 vol. hydrogen peroxide diluted by half. Then apply whatever powder or ointment the vet has prescribed.

INJURIES TO THE LOCOMOTIVE SYSTEM

WOUNDS

Wounds are of infinite kind, in shape, origin and gravity. Their seriousness should be determined by the condition of the wound and its position: torn and dirty tissue is much more serious than a deep, clean cut which is safe from infection. Cats wounds quickly grow septic and can be very serious especially near the joints.

Treatment: a) Superficial wounds: disinfect with pure water or mercurochrome. Cut the hair away all round, making sure that the fur does not get into the wound and be a further source of infection. Apply an ointment or antiseptic powder, then a gauze dressing (not cotton wool) held by plaster so that the cat cannot lick the wound. If the wound was dirty, change the dressing every twelve hours, cleaning and disinfecting every time.

b) Large, deep wounds: First disinfect with pure water or mercurochrome and remove any foreign bodies; then take the cat to the vet, who will decide what treatment should be given and will stitch the wound if necessary.

c) Wounds near joints: These are always serious because they may cause traumatic arthritis. After disinfecting the wound as instructed above, take the cat to the vet.

d) Wounds caused by bites: These are often quite small but do not neglect them. They easily form large abscesses, because saliva is full of germs. Disinfect as above and administer an antibiotic to the wound.

e) Haemorrhages: These may be the result of severed veins or arteries and their gravity depends on the position of the wound. If a vein has been cut the blood will be dark red; if an artery, the blood will be brilliant red, and it will gush out. Call the vet immediately and while waiting apply a tourniquet—of rubber or a strip of cloth—above the bleeding point, pull it as tight as you can if it is possible to bind the wound. If not, make a compress of cotton wool and gauze and apply it to the wound, holding it firmly in place either with the hand or a bandage.

SPRAINS

These are caused by tearing or pulling the ligament.
Symptoms: The cat limps and will not put its paw to the ground.
Treatment: Soak the limb in warm water. Then massage it gently with camphorated oil. The vet will give an injection to reduce inflammation and pain.

DISLOCATION

Dislocation of the bone at the joint.
Symptoms: The joint is deformed, the cat limps and is in great pain.
Treatment: Apply warm, damp compresses until the vet arrives. Only a qualified vet should attempt to put the bone in place. The animal will have to have a total anaesthetic. Then the limb will be set in plaster for as long as necessary.

FRACTURES

The most common are leg-fractures. They frequently occur in kittens, especially if they have rickets, and in aged cats where the bones are decalcified.
Symptoms: The cat will not put its weight on the broken leg, which moves unnaturally. There is intense pain.
Treatment: While waiting for the vet, immobilize the leg in a splint of corrugated cardboard held in position by a rubber band. When the fracture has been set, the vet will put the leg in plaster.

Wounds should never be ignored. They quickly become infected.

So much progress has been made in veterinary surgery that most fractures can be set, however bad the break. Surgical intervention, called osteosynthesis, which means putting the bones in place and pinning them with hooks, plates, screws or ligatures, has become common. It is usually very successful and, after a period of rehabilitation, your cat will have perfect use of its limbs.

BURNS

Burns are of two kinds: thermal burns caused by heat, and chemical burns caused by acids or alkalis.

a) *Thermal burns*
These are caused by boiling liquid such as water or oil, or by contact with something very hot.
The degrees shown below indicate their gravity.
1. *1st degree burns:* These are the least serious.
Symptoms: The skin is greatly irritated, red and sensitive; occasionally it forms into blisters exuding a yellow liquid.
Treatment: Apply mercurochrome or picric acid solution or sodium bicarbonate. Such burns leave no trace and the fur grows back in no time.
2. *2nd and 3rd degree burns:* The seriousness is determined more by their extent than their penetration. A 2nd degree burn over a large area is more serious than a small 3rd degree burn.
Symptoms: These burns are true wounds with serious oedemas. They usually cause a high temperature and exhaustion.
Treatment: Disinfect the wound with mercurochrome and call the vet who will dress the wound and give the cat hepatic preventatives, because reabsorption of burned tissue induces poisoning.
3. *4th degree burns:* This means carbonization of the skin. It is only found in animals that have escaped from a fire. Inhalation of fumes will also mean that

the respiratory membranes are much inflamed, probably resulting in chest complications. These are extremely serious cases and must be treated immediately by a vet who alone will be able to say whether the animal has a chance of survival.

b) *Chemical burns*
Such burns are caused by chemical products, acid or alkaline; they are always serious because they penetrate deeply into the tissue and the action may continue for a long time.
Rapid aid may help to reduce the damage.
1. *Acid burns: Benzene, turpentine, tar,* etc.
Treatment: Apply an alkaline solution all over: soapy water, bicarbonate of soda. It is important to lose no time.
2. *Alkali burns: Caustic soda, drain-cleanser, caustic potassium,* etc.
Treatment: Soak the wound with vinegar and water, boracic acid or a solution of picric acid.

BIBLIOGRAPHY

Aberconway, C., Lady. *A Dictionary of Cat Lovers,* Michael Joseph: London, 1968

Baker, Hettie Gray. *Your Siamese Cat,* Derek Verschoyle: London, 1952

Beachcroft, T. *Just Cats,* Country Life: London, 1936

Boorer, M. *Wild Cats,* Hamlyn: London, 1969

Carr, W. H. A. *The Basic Book of the Cat,* Stanley Paul: London, 1965

Clarke, F. E. *Of Cats and Men,* Macmillan Co.: New York, 1957

Crew, F. *All These and Kittens Too,* Herbert Jenkins: London, 1959

– *Devoted to Cats. A Book of Essays,* Frederick Muller: London, 1954

Darwin, Charles. *The Variation of Plants and Animals under Domestication,* London, 1868

Denis, A. *Cats of the World,* Constable: London, 1964. World Wildlife Series No. 1

Drew, E. and Joseph, M. *Puss in Books,* Dodd, Mead & Co.: New York, 1932

Eliot, T. S. *Old Possum's Book of Practical Cats,* Faber & Faber: London, 1939

Eustace, M. *The World of Show Cats,* Pelham: London, 1970

Eustace, M. and Towe, E. *The Royal Cat of Siam: the complete book of the Siamese Cat,* Pelham: London, 1968

Frazer, J. G. *The Golden Bough,* Macmillan: London, 1923

Gates, G. S. *The Modern Cat, her mind and manners. An Introduction to Comparative Psychology,* Macmillan Co.: New York, 1928

Gay, M. C. *How to Live with a Cat,* Reinhardt and Evans: London, 1949

Gray, N. S. *The Boys,* Dobson Books: London, 1968

Herford, O. *The Rubaiyat of a Persian Kitten,* Bickers & Son: London, 1904. USA, 1905

Howey, Mary Oldfield. *The Cat in the Mysteries of Religion and Magic,* Rider & Co.: London, 1930

Iles, Gerald. *Magnificat,* W. H. Allen: London, 1964

Jennings, John. *Domestic and Fancy Cats,* L. Upcott Gill: London; Charles Scribner's Sons: New York, 1906

Jude, A. C. *Cat Genetics,* All Pets: London, 1955

Kirk, H. The Cat's Medical Dictionary, Routledge: London, 1956

Langton, N. and B. *The Cat in Ancient Egypt,* University Press: Cambridge, 1940

Manning, O. *Extraordinary Cats,* Michael Joseph: London, 1967

Marks, A. *The Cat in History, Legend and Art,* Elliott Stock: London, 1909

McCoy, J. J. *The Complete Book of Cat Health and Care,* Herbert Jenkins: London, 1969.

Mellen, I. M. *A Practical Cat Book for Amateurs and Professionals,* Scribner's Sons: New York, 1939

Mellen, I. M. *The Science and Mystery of the Cat,* C. Scribner's Sons: New York, 1949

Méry, F. *Just Cats,* Souvenir Press: London, 1957

– *The Life History and Magic of the Cat,* Paul Hamlyn: London, 1968

Metcalf, C. *Cats,* Paul Hamlyn: London, 1967. Sun Books: Melbourne

Montgomery, J. *Looking after your cat,* George, Allen & Unwin: London, 1964

Nichols, B. *Cats' ABC,* Jonathan Cape: London, 1960

Platt, C. *Things You Don't Know About Cats,* Andrew Melrose: London & New York, 1924

Pond, G. *The Observer's Book of Cats,* Fred. Warne: London & New York, 1959

– *Persian Cats,* W. & G. Foyle: London, 1963

– *Cats,* Arco: London, 1962

– *Complete Cat Guide,* Pet Library: New York, 1968

– *The Long-haired Cats,* Arco: London, 1968. American edition 1970

Repplier, A. *The Fireside Sphinx,* Gay & Bird: London; Cambridge, Mass., 1901

Rice, B. *The Other End of the Leash; the American Way with Pets,* Angus & Robertson: London, 1968

Silkstone, D. *Pedigree Cat Breeding for Beginners,* Cat Information Centre: London, 1969

Sillar & Meyler. *Cats Ancient and Modern,* Oliver & Boyd: Edinburgh, London, 1966

Simmons, A. F. *Famous Cats,* Elliot Right Way Books: Kingswood, 1957; London, 1966

Simms, K. L. *They Walked Beside Me,* Hutchinson: London, 1954

Soame, E. B. H. *Cats Long-haired and Short,* Methuen & Co.: London, 1933

Soderberg, P. M. *Pedigree Cats, their Varieties, Breeding and Exhibition,* Cassell & Co.: London, 1958

Spies, J. R. *Cats and how I photograph them,* Studio & Thomas Cromwell: New York & London, 1958

Tenent, R. *The Book of the Siamese Cat,* Barrie & Jenkins: London, 1968

Uzé, M. *Le Chat dans la Nature, dans l'Histoire et dans l'Art,* Paris, 1951

Van Vechten, C. *The Tiger in the House,* William Heinemann: London, 1920; New York, 1921; Jonathan Cape: USA, 1938

Vezey-Fitzgerald, B. *Cats,* Penguin: London, 1957

Whitney, L. F. *The Complete Book of Cat Care,* Gollancz, London, 1953

Williams, K. R. *Siamese Cats,* W. & G. Foyle: London, 1960

Wilson, K. *A to Z of Cats,* Max Parrish: London, 1959

Winslow, H. *Concerning Cats, My Own and Some Others,* David Nutt: London, 1900. Norwood, Mass., 1903

ACKNOWLEDGMENTS

The illustrations reproduced are from the following sources:

A.C.L., Brussels: p. 69 (property of the Belgian Government)
Albertina Foundation, Records of the Austrian Nationalbibliothek, Vienna: pp. 64, 73, 104
Alinari, Florence: p. 25
Toni Angermayer, Munich: pp. 153, 155, 156, 206
Simone Annoot, Ypres: p. 20
Archives photographiques, Paris: pp. 29, 86
Art and Architecture (drawing): p. 25
B. Arthaud, Grenoble: p. 34
Bibliothèque Nationale, Paris: pp. 19, 29, 40, 43, 46, 50, 53, 57, 58, 61, 66, 67, 88, 89, 94, 102, 105, 107, 110, 112, 233
Boudet-Lamotte, Paris: p. 36
British Museum, London: pp. 23, 31, 32, 96, 125, 126, 127, 129, 130, 131, 133, 136, 139, 143, 145, 147, 148, 159
Josée Broueil-Nogué: p. 16 (Copyright by Spadem, Paris, and Cosmopress, Geneva)
J.E. Bulloz, Paris: pp. 59, 77, 82
Burgerbibliothek, Berne: p. 113
Camara Press, London: pp. 186, 242 (photo by John Bridge)
Collections:
— Dario Boccara, Paris: p. 8
— Yves Jeanneret, Grandvaux: p. 211 (photo by M. Vuillemin)
— Edgar William and Bernice Chrysler Garbisch: frontispiece
— Private collection, New York: p. 117
J. Combier, Mâcon: p. 44 (Copyright by Spadem, Paris, and Cosmopress, Geneva)
Pierre Darré, La Clayette: p. 65
G.H. Dubascoux: pp. 162, 176, 241
Edita, Lausanne: p. 41
Hans Erni, Meggen: p. 120
John R. Freeman, London: p. 62

Gabinetto Fotografico Nazionale, Rome: p. 86
Giraudon, Paris: pp. 27, 35, 54, 87, 89, 115, 217; Lauros-Giraudon: pp. 55, 93, 108, 116; Garanger-Giraudon: p. 109
Gillette Grilhé, St-Légier: pp. 160, 171, 173, 199, 214
The Solomon R. Guggenheim Museum, New York: p. 118
E. Haller-Maslov: pp. 167, 216
Harlingue-Viollet, Paris: pp. 21, 114, 115, 122
T. Hassia, Paris: p. 103
André Held, Ecublens: p. 83
Kinette Hurni, Lausanne: pp. 91, 152, 156, 160, 169, 203, 208, 211, 212, 222, 223, 226, 227, 228, 231
Jacana, Paris: p. 167 (photos by F. Petter, John X. Sundance and Philippe Summ)
Keystone, Zurich: pp. 156, 204, 213, 219
Kunstmuseum, Zurich: p. 123
Landesamt für Denkmalpflege, Schleswig-Holstein: p. 162
Lelivert et Landrock: p. 30
A. Leroi-Gourhan: p. 14
London Museum, London: p. 106
Galerie Maeght, Paris: p. 122
Metropolitan Museum of Art, New York: p. 52
Musées des Antiquités Nationales, Saint-Germain-en-Laye: p. 7
Musée Historique Lorrain, Nancy: p. 75
Museum of Fine Arts, Boston. Tompkins Collection. Arthur Gordon Tompkins Residuary Fund: p. 110
North Carolina Museum of Art: p. 10/11
Carlo Orlandini, Modena: p. 15
R. Pedicini, Naples: p. 158
Petit Palais, Geneva: dust-jacket, p. 121
R.G. Phélipeaux, Auxerre: p. 45
Rapho, Paris: p. 151 (photo Yan), p. 205 (photo by Janine Niépce), p. 221 (photo by Zalawski)
Réunion des Musées Nationaux, Paris: pp. 22, 24, 26, 28, 32, 33, 35, 51, 90, 91, 100, 154

INDEX

248

INDEX OF STANDARD BREEDS

INDEX OF NUTRITION, HEALTH AND ILLNESS

48